Communication by design: a study in corporate identity

COMMUNICATION BY DESIGN

a study in corporate identity

JAMES PILDITCH

McGRAW-HILL

London · New York · Toronto · Sydney
Johannesburg · Mexico · Panama · Singapore

Published by

McGRAW-HILL Publishing Company Limited
MAIDENHEAD · BERKSHIRE · ENGLAND

07 094214 5

Contents

Preface

In all history there has never been a period of accelerating change like the present and the foreseeable future. People everywhere – businessmen and bankers no less than government, unions, and private citizens – face the imperative need to understand and adjust to meet these changes.

Among them is the shifting relationship between industry and its various publics. It brings a new impetus to the whole question of corporate communications.

This book attempts to describe how design can help these relationships and is, indeed, an integral part of them. While a central theme does run through it, the book has been created deliberately as a mosaic of experiences and theories, supported at every turn by practical case histories. The hope is that the reader will build his own awareness of the layers of interrelating complexities as he reads on, and form conclusions to suit his own circumstance.

Writing this book, the author has sought the help of a number of organizations and designers in the United Kingdom, in the Common Market and EFTA countries, and in the United States. Their help has been most generously given, and the author wants to thank them.

Thanks are also due to Karen Munck who designed the cover, Geoffrey Gibbons and Peter Kerr who laid out the illustrations, Jennifer Lambton who wrote hundreds of letters and helped in other ways, and Penny Walbrook who typed the book in draft and final form.

JAMES PILDITCH

1

Communication conveys information

Throughout history, organizations and individuals have employed visual devices to help people recognize them better. Indeed, before men could read and write they used symbols to distinguish their goods from those of competitors. Brickmakers in Egypt, it is said, placed their mark on each brick they made. Soapmakers in ancient Rome were fined for selling unbranded soap. Flemish tapestry workers, could have one of their hands cut off for failing to mark their work. The Guilds had their emblems, noblemen their heraldry, the army its regimental badges and banners, religions their symbols. The military, indeed, show plainly enough how badges not only identify troops but may become a focus for loyalty, pride, courage, fear. The crucifix, swastika, hammer-and-sickle, are evidence enough of the power of symbols. All arouse emotions instantly.

In business, too, the use of symbolism has been growing for a century or more, although the role has shifted. Following the Industrial Revolution, when success went to the men who harnessed the most machines, an owner displayed on his letterhead a drawing of the 'works'. (This pride of production produced its own opposite in time. Often a modern communication goal is to make industry less mechanical, more human.) Some old symbols are still going strong. The three-pointed star of Mercedes-Benz was designed, so legend says, by Gottlieb Daimler, who died in 1900. The main works at Unterturkheim and the Marienfelde works both carried the three-pointed star at the front of the radiator cowls from 1911 on. Apart from a minor modification in 1926, when they merged with Benz, there has been no alteration since. The Zeiss camera mark has been in use since 1903. London Transport's famous symbol was introduced in 1914. There are other examples. Many, created years ago, have been modified gradually as time passed. Shell's pecten was first introduced in 1900, but today's universally known mark is quite unlike its original shape, and it is still being modified.

Today, one can point to a number of organizations that are recognized instantly wherever they appear. Volkswagen, the Red Cross, Pan Am, all have visual images that have been built patiently over a long time. Others, established more recently (the Campaign for Nuclear Disarmament, Nabisco, the Chrysler pentastar) became known quickly through the weight of end-lessly repetitive promotion.

Even though the idea is not new, the whole subject of corporate identity is attracting new interest throughout industry. Pioneers have a head start, but their ideas are being adapted and adopted everywhere. This interest is not confined to industry. Banks, insurance companies, local government, all manner of organizations now see the need to clarify their communications. Nor is this restricted to large groups. In some circumstances, the smaller the organization the more it needs all the modern devices it can muster to com-municate effectively. The head of a small Rotterdam import agency once said:

> All companies feel the need to improve the clarity and effectiveness of their communications. This is just as necessary for small companies as for large ones . . . ours is a small company, but it is growing quickly. We are convinced that a high quality of design, attached to all our activities, will speak well for us and further improve our competitive position.

Case histories throughout this book show this view is widely held.

Two points must be made at once. First, the true function of corporate communication policies is changing swiftly to match our own rapidly developing industrial and social environment. New concepts and new tech-niques are enlarging the basic understanding of this subject. Second, it is important to bear in mind that, while this work is handled by designers, it is not only design work. Important though they are, the criteria of graphic design are not the only ones to apply to what are, above all, questions of communication.

This must be stressed because, so often, what one sees and hears on this subject is misleadingly simplified. Policies that suit one firm are seldom right for another. Examples in this book will show that communication goals must always be specific to the organization, and vary extremely from company to company.

The bakery division of J. Lyons & Co., giant British food firm, for example, found that people thought of Lyons as too big, impersonal, and unfriendly. One of the reasons for their new visual identity was the need to be seen as smaller and more 'human'. This goal, diligently followed through, is at odds with the often-repeated and oversimplified urge for massive global communications, or with management's natural desire to have the true size of its company widely known.

While virtually all organizations of all kinds need to appraise their communications policies, there exists no panacea. What may be good for one may be bad for another. One must deplore the attitude that if a firm is well known it must be a good firm: Hitler was known well enough. This exposes a new dimension to the problem, a dimension which this book will explore.

As forcefully, one should warn against the often heard point of view that if a company projects good taste (perhaps following a visitation from a designer) then it is communicating efficiently.

It is important not to take the subject of corporate identity at face value, but to delve well into it. Two primary questions bring about a fallout of others:

1. Why is change from existing behaviour necessary?
2. Why is visual design involved in modern communications?

Industry has been spending considerable sums of money for a long time on what it rightly calls 'communications'. There is an annual expenditure of about £440 million in Britain on advertising, and £80 million on public relations. Leading firms have healthy budgets for employee relations. They paint their vehicle fleets, and have signs, flags, badges, ties, and the rest. The point is, though, that attitudes to, and organizations for, communication in many firms were often created for conditions which are quite unlike the present. They are inadequate for the future. Men in the world's advertising, public relations, and employee relations departments are aware of the need for change, and increasingly find themselves trying to handle modern situations without the resources to do so. Many firms do not have the organization to deal with their communications problems effectively simply because they have failed to identify the changes going on around them.

Processing information is becoming a predominant feature in business: receiving information on which to base decisions, and conveying information on which decisions can be made by customers, shareholders, employees, voters, bankers, and others. In certain senses, therefore, corporate success will come to depend on the skill with which management understands and deals with the problems of communication.

We should remind ourselves of two essentials. First, communication is about the flow of information, and information consists of facts. This statement, while simplified (there is more to communication than bare fact), is an early, important qualification. This book will suggest that effective communications include nuances of impressions, attitude, opinion, which should not be neglected; nonetheless, to state the essential component of *fact* is deliberate. Everyone experienced in this field knows organizations of all kinds that try to change their face without changing their facts. Lasting success cannot be achieved this way.

If we're anxious to communicate facts we have to ask: 'What facts?' Presumably, these must be facts that will, in the long or short run, have a beneficent effect on the organization. If one then asks: 'What kind of facts are they likely to be?' part of the answer must be: 'It depends who you are talking to, what action they can take to help you, and what will influence them to take that action.' A good deal more than uniformity and good taste, or even weight of appropriation, is involved in effective communication.

The second point is just as pertinent. Communication is a two-way street. Not only is it important to find out what people want and what information is likely to influence them favourably, it is necessary to determine how the flow of information is being received, and to what extent it is being acted on.

We can't begin to answer these questions unless we have some understanding of our changing world.

The bulk of this first chapter will throw out a random selection of examples of change to establish the point that old attitudes to audiences, or to communicating with them, almost certainly need reassessing.

A number of distinguished sociologists have attempted to explain facets of this change. Each, in his way, casts a light so blinding that we cannot help seeing the new world as quite unlike the one it replaces. The sum of their writing is that the world ahead of us is not just a logical progression from the past. It will be, and is already, different in kind. President de Gaulle once said:

> The world is undergoing a transformation to which no change that has yet occurred can be compared, either in scope or rapidity.

In all recorded history it is hard to think of a period of more radical change than the one we are now living through. When the Romans left England after 500 years, the darkening must have been intense. The Russian Revolution has already had an effect on history. But can even these equal the change that has occurred in Europe and America these last 30 years?

Units of all kinds are growing larger: towns, industries, bureaucratic institutions are all merging and developing to vast new proportions. As sociologist C Wright Mills has said:

> The small shop serving the neighbourhood is replaced by the anonymity of the national corporation: mass advertising replaces the personal influence of opinion between merchant and customer. The political leader hooks up his speech to a national network and speaks . . . to a million people he never saw and never will see.

One effect of this, according to David Riesman, professor in the department of Social Relations at Harvard University, is an increased sense of loneliness (witness the increasing mental illness ascribed to this) or a lack of 'belonging'. In his book *The Lonely Crowd*,[1] Professor Riesman shows how people build their own response to this. He traces how a new kind of man has emerged in Western society. Not learning from his parents or any authority, nor being guided by any in-built standards of conduct, he is influenced only by those he thinks his peers, the group he 'belongs' to. The significance of James Dean and Elvis Presley was that they were the first of the new 'peer group'. When

John Lennon said the Beatles were more important than Christ, he was being less blasphemous than perceptive. One does not wish to misrepresent Professor Riesman's penetrating book by distilling it into one sentence, but simply to suggest that we cannot hope to communicate effectively with people unless we understand them. Old attitudes won't do.

It is an irony that the people most conscious of human change, who mourn the loss of 'standards', and 'the decline in morals', are often those least prepared to change their methods to accommodate the rising generation.

There are a host of other changes altering essentially the society we live and work in. A number of these changes must be relevant to any book about communication.

Rising standards of education, the prosperous equality brought about by modern political systems, the collapse of boundaries of all kinds, and growing youthful populations (half the population of the United States, West Germany, Switzerland, the Netherlands, and doubtless elsewhere is under thirty; and getting younger; by 1971, Americans in their twenties will outnumber those in their thirties by seven to five). This must influence what a corporation says, and to whom.

The Western world is now an urban society. Nearly 75 per cent of the people who live in Britain live in cities, as do 70 per cent of Americans. The continuing trend is two way: people moving into town to seek work (and from smaller towns to more important centres); towns are sprawling further over the countryside. Only half jokingly, the writer James Cameron looked ahead to a Britain in 1978 when 'the corruption of the cities, already incurable by the sixties, was now complete'. All South-east England, from Harwick to Hampshire, St Albans to the sea, was absorbed in what he called the 'Metroland Megalopolis'. Looking further and writing more seriously, Herman Kahn and Anthony Weiner of the Hudson Institute talk of the great cities of Boshwash, Chipitts, and San-San sprawling from Boston to Washington, Chicago to Pittsburgh, and San Francisco to San Diego.

All this is in the future. But a recurring theme of this book is to shape corporate communications to be effective in the future. Even today, the trends are obvious and have already uprooted many people. How does it affect their attitudes to the modern corporation?

Most people no longer live near their work and most firms no longer can be in close touch with their customers in the way local businessmen have been for centuries. What bearing has this on employee attitudes? How does it influence what shoppers think of the corporation they buy from?

On the face of it the answers are simple. As workers cease to live in the shadow of their factory their loyalty to it diminishes. The need grows to build loyalty by other means. From this assumption, the corporation could draw conclusions and take decisions. Loyalty to class or race or school diminishes as distinctions crumble. Loyalty to one's country declines as boundaries melt. Curiously, it may be that the corporation or, at an executive level, profession, is becoming the new focal point for self-identification.

This is noticeable in the big international companies. A Unilever man may be a Unilever man first and a resident of Rotterdam, London, New York, or Paris second. He will often be more at home with a Shell man than with a compatriot in a smaller business. While paternalism is fiercely resisted, there exists a new opportunity to communicate effectively with people. In one sense, there is also a new need: to provide sheet-anchors in an increasingly uncertain world. This decline of loyalties influences people in the purchasing and consumer role, too.

Equally, the spread of business makes the problems of 'feedback' greater. The local businessman is not only known to his customers and workforce but he knows them.

Speaking to a symposium organized in New York by the Foundation for Research on Human Behaviour, Gerhart D Wiebe, from Boston University, pointed out that 'Mr Big' in the local community is:

acutely aware that his welfare derives from the general vigour, health and prosperity of the community. [He illustrated this:] If the town water supply was contaminated, his family was exposed to infection. If the schools were shoddy, his children would not qualify for university. If the farmers allowed their land to erode, mortgages would default and retail business would diminish. In a small community cause and effect are visibly connected.

The local trader is very directly concerned with the well-being of his community. He sits on committees, he knows a lot about the hopes, plans, and capabilities of his customers.

But what do you do when the whole population is your market? You have to send out information. But sending out information doesn't necessarily mean it is received; nor does receiving information necessarily mean it is understood and will lead to changed attitudes.

John W Riley Jnr[2] said at a conference in New York:

A corporate image is of little value without continuing and systematic information which tells the manager something of the extent to which the image is received and accepted by the various publics to which it is addressed.

Obviously the scale of events alters the problem radically, so that size creates *different* problems. For example, when the personal link breaks down (both as a result of distance and as management teams replace the single powerful man) the modern corporation has the task of finding some kind of equivalent by which people interested in the company can judge its performance, and people not interested can be attracted to a company.

Research has demonstrated that, apart from a few consumer-goods firms, people have very little knowledge of industry. Survey after survey reveals that even people who claim to know about a firm find it difficult to name a single executive in the company, or to list more than one or two of its

This chart, created by Dr Rudolph Beck, shows how visual communications and industrial design fit into the interrelationship of industry and art, technology and communications.

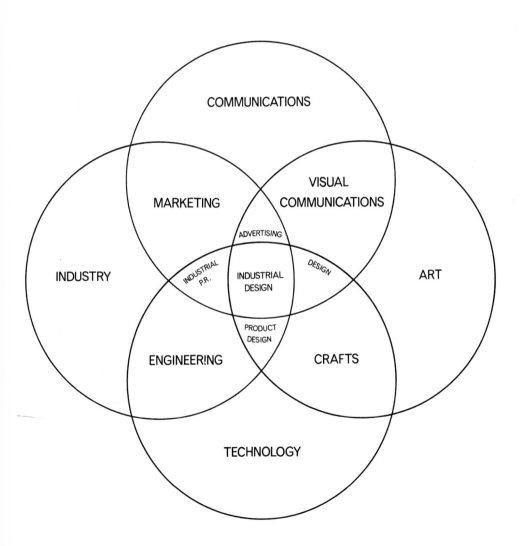

products. They have little or no knowledge of turnover, or labour relations, or any of the facts about which a company may feel proud. Further, they have little interest. So to spend a lot of time and money pronouncing that one's company is the biggest maker of computers or the fastest-growing supplier of radios may be a waste if people are not interested in either.

This bears on a good deal of what has been called 'prestige' advertising. Many firms spend money to establish a position of prestige beyond their obvious commercial needs. In product profitability terms, hardly anyone actually needs to locate his offices in Mayfair or on the Faubourg St Honoré, though the decision to move there may appear sound. Large sums can be wasted on prestige promotion that gets no one anywhere.

Realizing that consumers are not very interested in industry unless it impinges directly on them, we are forced to consider new ways of projecting the company. The Bull affair in France, the AEI-GEC merger in Britain, cancelling the TSR 2, all attracted public interest because they threatened the jobs and security of many people. Though more frequent as industry gets larger and as governments intervene in industry, such cases are still relatively rare. Much more usual is a lack of concern. In 1967, Kaiser Aluminium & Chemical Corporation published a 200-page book called *The Dynamics of Change*. Illustrated with over 50 full colour plates, it is a costly and deliberate attempt to provide an intelligent public with information and opinions. There is only the lightest reference to the sponsoring company. Seen in the old light of either commercial reality or prestige promotion, the book appears extravagant and misguided. Considered, however, as a means of creating a favourable climate for the company among an uninterested public, it rates high.

There are clear signs that as industry intrudes more on the lives of people, measuring their every gesture, the more aware general audiences become of business. A rash of novels set in the boardroom shows a desire to peer behind the curtains of big business, although this in no way implies approval.

There are conclusions to draw from this: perhaps the modern corporation should identify its audiences and itself with those things people are interested in: schools, peace, health, and so on. Channels of communication must be used for more than the usual escalating superlatives.

The corporation itself is changing. The economist, Kenneth Galbraith, has described how power in the large organization of any kind has shifted from the pinnacle to the middle. One might add that the marketing concept and new communications systems have changed the corporation from an inward-looking, vertical pyramid to an outward-oriented collection of circles, with management clustered around the middle. Marshall McLuhan believes that the speed of electric communications, a central theme of his writing, does not centralize power. In his view, it decentralizes. The speed of electric communications 'permits any place to be the centre'. This evidently has an influence on the shape of the modern company and on its communication policies. For a range of reasons, change from existing patterns of attitude and behaviour towards corporate communications is overdue.

Modern sociologists lend powerful support to the designers who have been urging industrialists to treat their visual identities with care, and to take a total approach to the whole question of communication. For some years designers have argued that it is not only the formal channels of communication (TV advertising, employee notice boards, and annual reports) that influence attitudes. Examples abound of sparkling advertisements projecting carefree consumers inhabiting a world of plenty thanks to the kindness and amazingly advanced research of the sponsor. Some of these advertisements emerge from companies that have Queen Anne offices, cramped factories, dirty vehicles, and anything but the blandness they portray. This is the blinkered approach. Consumers display less and less intention of accepting anything uncritically. They no longer just take what's given to them. The modern corporation depends for survival on many diverse groups of people. It must stand up to their scrutiny from any aspect. That is one reason for taking a total view of corporate communications, so that the same message may be received wherever contact with the firm is made. A second is that the changing scale of markets and rising costs of promotion make it increasingly difficult to maintain contact with the right audiences. From this point of view alone it makes sense to combine all one's resources to project messages consistently. And there is a third, more fundamental, point.

In his book *Understanding Media*,[3] Marshall McLuhan claims that:

> more and more we turn from the content of messages to study their total effect. [He maintains that this effect] involves the total situation and not a single level of information movement.

Far from being an adjunct of advertising, corporate communications have become the new total – of which advertising is a part. Advertising, like public relations, architecture, merchandising material, and any part of a company's outpourings, must be coordinated with the rest so that each contributes to one appropriate whole.

This is self-evident, but seldom done. IBM is one of very few companies with a communication division, but even this excludes products and buildings. Offices of corporate identity are being set up in a number of companies, but the board of Shell International, otherwise sophisticated in these subjects, judged that their 43-acre building dominating the skyline by the Thames in London is 'not a visible manifestation of the company' and, therefore, did not involve the executives responsible for their corporate look. EL AL, too, is remarkable. By a most enlightened policy, George Him, an independent consultant, is responsible for all visible manifestations of the airline – except advertising. The reason for this fractured approach expresses itself in the departmentalized organization of a company, but really lies deeper – in a failure to recognize the need to be seen and understood *from all points of view*.

Glancing at the history of art, which has often predicted the evolution of seeing and understanding, it is interesting to remember that cubism, fifty years ago, shattered the traditional and formal attitude that people saw things from one vantage-point only. Picasso was among the first to create pictures that allowed viewers to have an instant awareness of the whole. He'd paint a woman from the front and side at the same time. His famous painting of the Spanish Civil War, 'Guernica', threw onto an enormous canvas everything that tells of the horror of the first bombing of a civilian population. He saw that modern man needs to understand the whole scene, and is no longer satisfied to have a vantage-point chosen for him.

It is fascinating to see this reflected in modern film making where one may occasionally see half a dozen separate images, all fractions of the total, on the screen at one time. One meaning of this is that conveying information need no longer be a linear process. Different facets of a story can be conveyed simultaneously.

The case for a total approach to communications (though recognizing that there are optimum levels for this) is incontestable. To rely on the formal channels of contact between manufacturer, distributor, and purchaser is not enough. Neither does the solution lie simply in increasing the weight of effort through these direct channels. It is no good asking people to believe what they are told when the evidence before them tells them otherwise. Equally, it is absurd to ignore ways of conveying impressions that are at least as trusted as the advertisements and displays now created to do this job.

The case for visual communications scarcely needs making, particularly now when our visual senses have been so sharpened by television. Ours has become a visual world.

One of the most important differences between parents and children today lies in the fact that children, brought up with TV, learn visually. But the strength of visual communications has always been there. Children draw before they write. It may be true that educationalists have neglected the visual senses. People have been taught the language of words and numbers, but seldom the language of vision, but ample evidence exists of the power to communicate in visual terms.

Friso Kramer of Total Design in Amsterdam puts it differently:

> Good design is something people need. You need design as you need art. People can't live without it.

For social and commercial reasons the problem has changed. To meet this new situation communication, and all-round communication at that, must become a central preoccupation of management.

This works several ways. Today's employees are accustomed to greatly improved standards of consideration and comfort. Not only must corporations recognize this, they must be seen to recognize it. People want – and have the strength to seek – more than a pay packet. They need an interest, a sense of purpose and identification. As traditional ideas of control by discipline are revised, the company must develop in its staff the self-discipline that comes

One of these shapes is associated with the word 'MALUMA', the other with the word 'TACKETA'. Which is which? The chances are you connect the round shape left with the smooth-flowing word 'Maluma' and the sharper shape with the word 'Tacketa'. This suggests that there is a correlation between even abstract sounds and symbols, and that to communicate most effectively one should consider both as expressions of the same idea.

from individual identification with corporate goals. We can only expect people to work for corporate goals if they understand them and approve of them. This is as true of the switchboard girl as of the senior executive.

Staff and workers see a company closest: they are the company. Yet the company is more than the people in it. To have considerately designed offices, branches, and workshops undoubtedly influences the attitudes of workers to the company.

This is true, too, of the endless search for good staff. One sees generous financial inducements, pay, security, pensions, holidays, profit-sharing, which still stop short of realistic understanding of staff problems: all these are not enough if people don't *like* where they work, or don't see any value in what they are paid to do.

Outside the company too, good communication matters. It is true, sadly, that often poor images exist which adversely influence attitudes to the company. These damaging images may be quite undeserved, the result of neglect and ignorance more than of bad practice. The modern corporation depends for existence on the people who work for it and the public buying from it. But it depends, too, on a maze of other relationships: with government, planning authorities, local councils, trade associations, distributors, dealers, families of company staff, shareholders, bankers, suppliers, newspapers, magazines, and television.

It is impossible to be unaware of the influence of these widespread audiences. It is no longer sufficient to treat them in uncoordinated ways. Impressions conveyed verbally must marry those conveyed visually. And both must equal reality. How to determine that reality and convey it effectively in our changing world is the purpose of this book.

There's one question to ask: shouldn't a book about corporate identifications be confined to graphic design, and particularly the design of symbols? While in this book we show a number of cases that use symbols to advantage, it is wrong to so restrict one's thinking. Not everyone agrees with designer F H K Henrion when he says 'there should be a great anti-symbol campaign', but there is a point in his comment. (He believes big companies may benefit from them, but smaller companies simply increase the confusion.)

Mike Bochna of the Compagnie d'Esthétique Industrielle in Paris, the design office which handled BP's corporate identity problems for seven years, has pointed out that a corporate identity can range all the way from a graphic solution to a total attitude affecting the corporation's graphics, physical manifestations, and even its philosophy. And it is this total approach which will furnish the background for our comments on design.

REFERENCES

1. Yale University Press, 1950.
2. Author of *The Corporation and its Publics*, Wiley, 1963.
3. Routledge & Kegan Paul, 1964.

2

New ways to look at brand *v.* corporate identity

In the face of competition for recognition from among thousands of organizations, one can only hope to be fully known if every possible aspect of a company bears the same identity. This is a plea for coordination and simplicity. But, by itself, this is not enough, and this chapter and later ones explore the problems that can arise. For example, how coordinated should a company's visible manifestations be when it works to a 'brand' concept? When a company is international, is it right to have the same image everywhere or should the aim be to suit each local market? Within a group, should all divisions or companies look alike, or should they vary to suit their functions?

These few questions show the complexity of the subject. There is more to proper visual communication than just placing a new symbol nicely on international-size paper.

The prerequisite must be to decide what the organization should communicate. No organization can be all things to all people; neither are all ideas equally helpful to it. Selection is required.

An example of this arose when the David Brown Corporation developed and tested a number of new symbols. The corporation, the second largest private company in the UK, makes Aston Martin cars, tractors, gears, ships, electronic equipment, and hovercraft. A characteristic throughout these diverse activities is advanced high-quality engineering. The symbol research revealed a clear split. People interviewed thought the existing symbol represented a friendly, small, and somewhat old-fashioned firm. One of the new symbols was seen as representing the opposite – a thrustful, advanced, big, modern firm – but less personal and friendly. Which was the best choice? They chose the 'advanced' symbol.

Smiths Food Group faced the same kind of decision. Long established as Smiths Potato Crisps, they were part of the English scene – as English as the pubs their crisps were bought in. To change this image, so thoroughly well known, might have been thought risky. But their market changed. Crisps were being bought increasingly in supermarkets, bought by mothers and consumed by children aged between six and twelve. Smiths revamped their image to appeal to this new market, at the expense of their famous past. Interestingly, the results were instantaneous. Sales increased substantially within a month of the launching of the new image. Reaction from the trade was enthusiastic.

There was a further turn to the story. Within a month, General Mills, the US giant, announced its intention to acquire all the shares of Smiths. At once the company's basic position changed. A new situation arose calling for great skill. As an American company in Britain, Smiths now became vulnerable to any and all anti-American feeling. As US investment in Europe increases, this is a prejudice to reckon with. This was made clear the day control was gained: TV newscasts showed the Smiths' takeover immediately before film of strikers objecting to US methods in a factory in Lancashire.

A company's long-term success could well be influenced by the way it handles this kind of communication problem. This story illustrates another truth of corporate communications: that this is a dynamic, changing subject. The market changes, the company changes, social attitudes alter. At no time can one relax in the certain knowledge that a corporate identity policy is right for years ahead.

Every corporate identity requires choice. Which, of many potentially favourable facts are the ones most likely to benefit an organization? Are there negatives to overcome? Are the same essential facts of the same value to different firms?

There are no simple solutions, which is probably just as well. If all companies aimed at the same magic formula, there would be endless confusion of identities. Companies, starting from the same point, grow in different ways: even major competitors in the same product field have differences of outlook, strengths, and weaknesses in different areas.

The important basis of all corporate communications is a statement of communication goals. Before redesigning or rewriting anything, it is worth asking a few fundamental questions, which in itself, can be a valuable exercise.

The questions should strike both inwards and outwards, and be related later. Consultant designers appointed to the task conduct the questioning and write their recommendations. Their objectivity suits them to this role.

Within the company, they want to know what the company does, where it has come from, and where it is going to. What is the fundamental purpose of the company? The answer to this is seldom as elementary or obvious as executives in the company suppose. In *Understanding Media* McLuhan wrote:

14

It is only today that industries have become aware of the various kinds of business in which they are engaged. When **IBM** discovered it was not in the business of making office equipment or business machines but that it was in the business of processing information, then it began to navigate with a clear vision.

It is interesting to ask executives and staff in a company what they think of it. Everyone has his ideas of the problems facing his organization and can propose the kind of image the company should portray. They may not always be right, but simply by being in the company their views have the authority of practical experience. They will have to live with whatever is decided.

Talking individually to people, one recognizes areas of agreement and of conflict. At first they tend to generalize, want the company to be seen as possessing all the virtues, but by pursuing each word to its logical conclusion, the list of desirable attributes shortens, and becomes more specifically related to company needs.

This questioning must certainly include the most senior officers of the company. One must know the company's aims. Will it decentralize? Will it diversify? Will it be internationally established? Will there be mergers? All these points effect a recommendation. Time is another factor. In any big company it takes years to bring about a complete change (for cost reasons if no other), and for a new corporate communication policy to be fully effective. One must look ahead a long way, to the future environment in which any new scheme must work.

From questioning within a company the consultant designer can get a picture of the company and its problems, its strengths and weaknesses, the power of its organization and its long-range intentions. This is essentially a slanted, perhaps flattering, view. For this reason it is necessary to find the attitudes towards the firm from people outside it – such as suppliers, whole-salers, and distributors. These may show that the company's deliveries are slow, that its pricing policy is always changing, or that its telephone service is inefficient. The problems of these outside agencies, in turn, reflect on the corporation.

A recent example of this concerned Van Gelder Papier, the largest paper manufacturer in the Netherlands. Their size had led to inertia. Evidence revealed by enquiry showed that while buyers thought the company's products good and often the best available, they complained of late deliveries. New management fought hard for change and a particular drive was made not only to improve service, but to emphasize that the 'new' company (its name was altered as evidence of change) placed great emphasis on good service.

A British food firm may be quoted as another example. As part of a general drive to strengthen and improve its communications, the design consultants advised that discount arrangements should be published. Previously, even though the discount structure was much the same for everyone, it was kept secret, believing that the sales manager held an advantage in being able to give, or appear to give, better terms to certain customers as an added inducement to buy. Part of the reason for recommending that consistent terms should be published was to make it clear to the trade that the company was fair – and large enough not to make exceptions. Thus, the discount policy was altered partly to suit the communication goal.

It is extraordinary how often the trade is overlooked when corporate design policies are put into effect. This can only be a mistake.

Equally, many companies claim to be 'consumer-oriented' – but forget to consider the consumer when changing the face of the firm.

One terse definition of marketing, is: 'To provide consumer satisfaction at an acceptable profit to you and to the trade.' How may this best be done in image terms? The answer lies only partly in trying to determine what people want that you can provide, essential though this is. Bearing in mind that attitudes to companies are by no means as favourable or well informed as one would like, one must ask how the corporation can evoke satisfactory responses from the general public.

What do people think of your industry? What qualities will incline them favourably to your organization? In the short term, what characteristics, if associated with your company, will influence them to choose your products, buy your shares, apply to you for a job? In the long term, how may you best position your company, as regards image, so that it is accepted by people living in a different world?

And which people? Perhaps the single most obvious characteristic separating the effective, marketing-oriented company from the general run of industry is a sharp definition of its customers. Few companies can hope to appeal equally to all people all the time. Definition of which groups of people influence a company is central to purposeful communication. This goes far beyond the obvious socio-economic or geographical analysis, but plunges into the psychology of people.

In all these questions, consumer research can, and has often, revealed situations of immediate help; but there must be speculation. Again, one must look forward a long way: an intelligent review of social trends and technological development can lead to workable postulations.

An example of the first was provided by research conducted for Albert Heijn, the Dutch supermarket chain. It showed that while the company was extremely well known and admired, it was thought too aggressive. An immediate communication goal was to soften this attitude – in fact as well as fancy – to place the company as modern and clean, and forward-looking, without the harsh aggressiveness that had been associated with it.

When two Belgian biscuit companies merged, long-term postulation became necessary. The two companies were almost equally dominant in their market. They formed a single company with a new name, which was fine as far as it went. But what then? Should they forget the old names and build the new? Choose one name and ignore the other? Relate both old names to the new company? And what about the new name: didn't it sound like another US takeover? How should that be handled?

To answer such questions, the design consultants not only looked at the current situation with care, but tried to see ahead, to the possible evolution of the EEC and to other factors bearing on the company. The result was a weighty document. Among the points discussed was that freshness is vital to bakery products. It may be argued, therefore, that the best (i.e., freshest) biscuits are baked locally, so no time is lost in transportation (modern packaging, in fact, weakens this argument). This would suggest that the company should have local bakeries in the regions and countries it serves.

On the other hand, 'local' probably equals 'small'. The designers hypothesized that many very large firms are growing in Europe and that they will probably make it their business to put across the reliability and efficiency that size brings. People may come to accept, more and more, the overall advantage of buying from big and famous firms. It happens that these companies are often either American or British. It is also true that British biscuits are thought to be good, and that American food firms are respected for their cleanliness and modernity. If this line of thought were to prevail, it was argued, then the somewhat Anglo-Saxon name would fit it well.

Combining this conclusion with others, the company decided to use the former names as brand names, and to bring up the new group name to underline the size of the company.

Each case quoted is more involved than the part extracted. This example shows that conjecture about the future is essential to corporate identity work, and that predictions can be specific to the company concerned.

By relating and sifting conclusions drawn from the company, those who deal with it, consumers, and trends in the industry and in society, one may arrive at a distillation of the true arguments. Deciding these correctly is of the utmost importance. It is at this point that the character of the company will be set. Moreover, this is of more than artistic interest: the company will have to live up to its propaganda.

One can underline this by quoting the typical dilemma of an airline. How do you project an airline? Is speed the most important factor that decides which airline you fly? The BOAC emblem is called a 'Speedbird'. Is worldwide coverage a factor? The Pan Am symbol is a globe. Do people want the thrill of being lifted above the clouds? TWA promotes an 'up, up, and away' message. Perhaps the size of the airline is important: small airlines may be thought unlikely to have the most expensive and advanced equipment, their standards may be thought lower – without justification. Or, for people bored with bureaucracy, the individual initiative of a small airline may be just what they're looking for.

Being big is not an unmitigated blessing; friendliness counts for a lot (Aer Lingus consistently project it) so long as it is not at the expense of efficiency.

Where do you put your priorities?

KLM Royal Dutch Airlines, found that people associate an airline with its nationality. Whether related to fact or not, the popular images of countries stick indelibly to their airlines. If the Dutch are thought of as reliable and hard-working, this is how KLM tends to be seen. France is associated with good food; people expect good food on Air France planes.

We know that some of these popular impressions are related to the qualities people seek when they fly. International regulations ensure that actual standards are satisfactory, but it is important for individual airlines to emphasize individual qualities and strengths.

The particular case of EL AL (in Hebrew it means 'upwards') is quoted here to show the thought that lies behind the basic determination of communication goals. According to George Him, the consultant designer, coordinator, and arbiter of design for EL AL, the image should change from country to country: 'In Finland we stress Mediterranean sun, in Italy something else.' Him selects local architects to work in each country. He is ready to sacrifice uniformity for personality, providing the same identity is projected.

The following notes taken from a general instruction he created, cover the building of new offices, and show how he has defined the airline's personality, and conveys it to others.

1. Theme

The main function of an EL AL office, outside its purely practical performance, is to give the prospective traveller *confidence* in the airline (many people are still afraid of travelling by air) and the *pleasurable anticipation* at the prospect of flying with this particular company.

EL AL is a reliable airline with a global reputation. At the same time, it is Israel's national carrier and, as such, represents its country and reflects its image. Obviously, both these aspects must find their expression in the design treatment of EL AL offices.

Whereas the airline aspect is self-evident, the Israeli one needs clarification as the image of the country itself is rather complex.

To the people outside, Israel appears to be:

(a) An ultra-modern state, characterized by efficiency, advanced technology, and dynamism.
(b) The country of an ancient race with a 4000-years-old tradition and one of the main contributors to world civilization.
(c) A young pioneering country, somewhat rugged, but hospitable and friendly.
(d) The heir of the Jewish tradition which dictates human warmth and personal interest in dealing with strangers.

(e) A tourist country where the old mixes with the new and east meets west. A country of ancient ruins and modern hotels; of rugged wilderness and green, newly reclaimed land; of sea, sunshine, and beaches.

However, while considering these positive aspects of Israel, it is also important to bear in mind certain apprehensions that may influence the prospective traveller:

(a) That, being a pioneering country, it may be primitive and lack western comfort.
(b) That there may be a lack of know-how in matters of service and organization.
(c) That improvisation and muddling-through would be substituted for real experience.
(d) That Israelis would not be able to afford equipment in line with true international standards.

All arguments for and against Israel will, quite naturally, influence the attitude of the public towards EL AL.

2. Suggested line of approach

(a) RELIABILITY
The dominant impression of an EL AL office should be one of super-efficiency and up-to-dateness with a strong technological note. This is of supreme importance in order to put the passenger's mind at ease regarding his personal safety – a subject looming largely in his imagination but one which must never be directly mentioned in the airline business.

(b) MODESTY
It is important to remember that Israel is a small and by no means rich country. Therefore, an office of the Israel Airlines must never be extravagant or exaggeratedly luxurious. A certain simplicity or even ruggedness of treatment, combined with very comfortable and perfectly finished furniture should be the aim.

(c) MEDITERRANEAN ASPECT
Israel is a hot, sunny country washed by blue seas. Hence, the interior of an EL AL office should be gay, warm, and friendly. This can be best achieved by colour scheme and lighting. It can be enhanced by the use of the ordinary Israeli cactus which has become a symbol of Young Israel and which can be easily supplied from Israel. Naturally, cacti can only be used in countries where they do not grow in the normal way.

(d) TRADITIONAL ASPECTS

Most Jewish EL AL passengers expect to find in an EL AL office some link with Jewish history and tradition; at the same time, the same elements may appeal to the non-Jew as unusual and, therefore, interesting.

Unfortunately, Jewish traditional elements are so closely connected with religious observance that they have acquired a sacral character which would be entirely out of place in the office of an airline of our technological age. Even the use of the mediaeval Hebrew lettering, familiar from the usual Bibles and Holy Scrolls, has very little in common with modern Israel, whose true link with the Biblical past lies in the revival of the language itself, and not in the characters evolved under the influence of European black-letter calligraphy.

On the other hand, modern Hebrew lettering which tries to revive letter forms of the Biblical age is ideally suitable, if used in a purely decorative way, to give EL AL offices the desired distinctive note. It is less ornate, the shapes are simpler and more geometric and can therefore fit much better into a contemporary architectural language.

(e) GLOBAL ASPECT

Air travellers have a marked preference for large airlines, as they expect better service from them. EL AL, without belonging to the really large companies, flies to eighteen countries in four continents. This, for the airline of one of the smallest countries of the world, is quite an impressive record. It is desirable to express it, even if it is merely in the shape of a list of destinations.

(f) FRIENDLINESS

EL AL prides itself on treating its passengers as people, and not as serial numbers. It wishes to offer warm, friendly, and personalized service. An EL AL office, therefore, must look friendly and inviting.

(g) GENERAL MOOD

The emotional impact of an EL AL office should be that of something young, gay, friendly, simple, comfortable, efficient, enterprising, progressive, *avant-garde*.

The instruction then goes into details of materials to use, company identification, and practical considerations – all seen as part of the whole. It is worth remembering that EL AL is one of the few airlines making a profit.

This expression of a corporate personality emphasizes that even within one industry there are always particular answers. The case shows, too, how the particular may be affected by the general.

The airlines provide interesting examples, too, of two widespread influences on corporate identity. First is the way particular organizations can be given the virtues of the country they come from. This can be a two-edged sword, to be treated with care. Second is the way the important and differentiating characteristics of organizations may be far from the product itself, or just aspects of the whole blown up to large proportions.

Canadian National Railways had been revitalizing themselves for ten years and yet a survey conducted by CN in 1959 showed that people still had a poor impression of the railway industry. It was regarded as old fashioned, slow to experiment, and unconcerned with improving its services. CN suffered from this even though they had spent many millions of dollars changing from steam to diesel, embraced centralized traffic control, and integrated data processing as well as anyone. But most of these changes were behind the scenes. When they employed designers, a central part of the brief was to 'give CN a distinctive, easily recognizable identity, making it stand out. . . .' One way to deal with the attitude to railways as a whole was to make sure CN was distinguished from the image as a whole. This point emerges in a number of cases quoted in this book.

The design programme, followed through with high quality, helped accomplish results. A study, made in 1966 by an independent firm, showed that (since the 1959 findings) CN had substantially improved its corporate image. It had

> enhanced its reputation in terms of being progressive, efficiently run, trying to serve the public well, providing for security and having good morale.

These two cases suggest that part of one's enquiry should be to look at attitudes to an entire industry. Before designing for *this* coal merchant, ask what people think about coal and *any* coal merchant.

The process which determines goals to aim at may be based on research of various kinds, but it must neglect neither executive judgement nor creative thought.

It is evident that the qualities being conveyed must exist. Cracks in the wall cannot be papered. Worthwhile firms will want to repair such cracks and if designers spot flaws they can be, and usually are, remedied. The problem is to judge which qualities will be most appropriate and helpful to the firm in years to come – in competitive and social conditions which do not yet exist.

This is a very important qualification. One is always thinking of the future if only because it takes time for identity programmes to work. Industry is recognizing the need to come closer to its markets, and to defining the problems of those markets. It is clear that the more one tries to solve such problems, the less one can specialize. Thus, many firms with clear, though narrow, definitions will find themselves needing to broaden, to take in wider services or more comprehensive 'systems' for customer satisfaction. From this one must say that to see the company as it stands today is to be provided with a guide to the future but maybe little more.

Charrington United Breweries asked themselves this question. They took an old Toby jug and simplified it to create a mark that has the qualities associated with English inns. Friendliness, warmth, a certain robust strength, tradition. This, with a characteristic letterstyle and colour scheme, was applied to the group's thousands of pubs. The same feeling was conveyed in advertising.

A design manual was published and sent to offices throughout the company, their architects, and others. After three years of implementation, the company asked the consultant designers to see what had happened. How well had the original scheme been handled in the regions? Were any changes necessary? Here was the wisdom of recognizing that corporate communication possesses and requires a dynamic if it is to stay fully effective.

The posture of a company depends not only on the company itself, its industry, markets, and environment, but also on its competitors and relationships. When a competitor holds a commanding position, one must decide whether to place oneself close to it in service and image or to structure oneself differently, with unique characteristics. But this latter course can only work when the difference is an acceptable one. There have been examples of companies so preoccupied with the USP (Unique Selling Proposition) theory that they have found and promoted uniqueness without wondering whether anyone wants it.

Extremes of this kind have been perpetrated. One sees companies that are so concerned with projecting 'right' images that they forget the obvious ones. As an example, it may be highly desirable for an engineering company to stand out from competitors by laying emphasis on its excellent research facilities, but to do this at the expense of its engineering qualities could be to mislead everyone.

There is much to be said for stating the obvious first.

The position of a firm *vis-à-vis* its competitors undoubtedly influences *what* the firm says and *how* the firm says it.

The three giants in the British biscuit business prefer a degree of anonymity at this time. Their member companies are promoted (Peak Frean, Crawfords, McVitie & Price, Huntley & Palmer, etc.), but the main corporate bodies are not as well known.

In this competitive environment, Elkes Biscuits, even though it is the largest privately owned biscuit and cake manufacturer in the UK, felt it could not afford the same tactics. It saw the need to do the opposite; to concentrate its identity, so that every package helps to establish the company. The subsidiaries have all been absorbed into the same strong communication of one identity.

The need to be specific can be illustrated by countless case histories. Here one need only say that the people concerned with corporate communications must be able to advise on and decide the specific attitude for the company to adopt.

There are four groups of situations at least in which this question can arise.

1. Situations concerning an individual organization making or providing essentially one type of product or service.
2. An individual company with a number of established brands.
3. An organization with a number of distinct operating divisions, or a group with a number of subsidiary companies.
4. An international organization or group.

Though all have much in common (and this can be applied equally to government departments and social services as well as to commerical corporations), the problems get more complex as we move from 1 to 4. They may also move progressively further away from day-to-day marketing requirements, but this does not minimize their value. An essential ingredient of corporate communication work is the planned effort to reach medium- and long-term goals. It must come as no surprise that this often conflicts with the short-term. Nonetheless, to resolve such conflicts is necessary. The long-term voice must be heard.

In each case it is important to decide what is the business of the organization, and then to pursue the questioning mentioned earlier. Again, one must stress that each case is specific and that generalizations are hard to make, even on such universal problems as the relation of brands to a corporation.

The brand concept is now widely accepted and, perhaps because the best examples are the soap companies where the brand philosophy is practised, is now closely identified with good marketing. It is not new. Unilever introduced the marketing concept in 1919. Equally, the brand concept is not always right.

Nonetheless, there are situations where the brand philosophy is effective. It is interesting to see motor cars being sold as brands. The Cortina launch was a brand launch. The Mini is much more a Mini than a product of Morris or Austin or British Leyland Motor Corporation.

The pertinent question is not when to adopt the brand policy, but how to see this in corporate terms. In the soap business, the archetypal product or brand structure, an important change is taking place.

Marketing men have thought in the past that the brand name was the important thing to get across. They felt that the company making the brand was unimportant, and didn't help sell the product. Who cares who makes Tide as long as Tide has what the shoppers want?

This view is now less strongly held. In front of the author now is a bottle of Square Deal Quix. Which is the brand name? In a prominent place it states: 'A Lever Product – guaranteed.' Below it is written: 'Lever quality and performance guaranteed or your money back.'

It is because Unilever have been so committed to one philosophy that this change commands our interest. Lever Brothers and Associates is but one part of the Unilever organization. Early in 1957 Unilever announced that they had retained British design consultants to review their corporate communication policies.

Without detracting from the brand philosophy, it is clear that various developments are causing people to think again. Part of the answer lies in the rising cost of launching and promoting new brands. If shoppers believe Lever Brothers is a good company selling good products they may more readily accept new products if they bear the Lever guarantee. One product, package, or advertisement will support another.

Another part of the answer is that in the detergent market, as in other fields, the profusion of apparently similar products makes it hard for consumers to choose between them. A trusted guarantee of quality can help. In this particular field, it is true that heavy brand promotion has led to mistrust of claims. A solid reassurance from a company that people trust, can offset this to some extent.

A corporation needs to become well known in the interests of attracting shareholders and employees, and developing good relations generally.

Three points emerge. First, the relationship between brand and corporate identity is being reassessed. Second, the requirements of a corporate identity are different from those of a brand. This difference must be understood and preserved, and, the problem of relating the two will then be much easier to solve. Third, relationships must vary to suit the situation, particularly the comparative strength of brand name to corporate name, the ubiquity of the corporate name, and the appropriateness of the product to the corporate identity.

You might say that Heinz is such a strong name that to introduce other names can only weaken a favourable impact. In the retailing field, the name of Sainsbury says enough about the quality and value of a product to make it a very important statement, not to be played down. This kind of reputation is harder to achieve for a multi-brandname company.

Increasingly, executives will want to relate a company more closely with the product it sells. Most companies try to do too much. They have more product and brand names than they can hope to project effectively.

The higher the costs of promotion and distribution rise, the more rationalization one may expect. The number of brand names will decline as the scale of competition gets bigger.

Maybe a multiplicity of names is needed and can be supported by the large organizations, but even they will combine and eliminate numbers of names in the next few years. They will concentrate at one level while smaller firms may concentrate at another level – by bringing up the corporate name and, in some cases, eliminating 'brand' names as far as possible.

While the need to concentrate pervades all modern industrial and governmental communications, the problems alter in the bigger company with distinct operating divisions, or in the group with subsidiary companies. Up to now ICI has identified itself equally in paint, pharmaceutical, and fertilizer marketing. But the public won't accept all such juxtapositions. Fisons is one of the biggest firms in Europe making fertilizer; it also sells food, pharmaceuticals, and cosmetics. Would it be right to put them all under the same banner? If one did, should the identification be more or less important than any brand identities that exist?

The bigger groups are getting bigger, and every merger creates the need to do something about corporate identity. As companies diversify, they dilute any impression they at present convey. It is hard to have a clear picture of the scope or function of a firm that is really 20, or 50, or 100 companies. This obviously affects external communication, and it also affects the internal organization.

The story is told of the way a company in a huge £260 million group lost a big order. When the local company boss was asked by an important potential customer how many employees there were in the firm, he replied, '350', forgetting the true *group* assets. The buyer, an East European government, thought this too small to provide the reliability or service required.

As acquisitions take place, the central group, often starting with fond ideas of loose control and lots of autonomy at the operating level, soon finds itself needing to coordinate functions. To make coordination effective, they need some control. This process seems to go on until the counter need is felt to put responsibility back nearer the market-place. At any time, some companies are moving to more central control, others to less. Even so, the communication policy prevailing today is undoubtedly towards greater unity, and that means greater coordination of local design and communication activity.

This does not necessarily mean losing the identity of member companies. It will mean that groups must take time to consider what their policies should be. Should member companies be related or not? If so, how closely? Tube Investments has seventy member companies. It has allowed them to keep their identities but, at the same time, requires that they all acknowledge and display membership of the group. To this end, designers were retained to establish standards for the consistent use of the group identity on all advertising, exhibitions, stationery, vehicles, and so on.

The David Brown Corporation did the same. But both companies have one thing in common. While they are diverse groups, each tends to concentrate in a certain area of operation. To relate them all makes sense.

Mitsubishi Shoji Kaisha is much bigger than either. Although there are no strict rules, all or most of their products carry the 'three diamond' symbol (that's what *mitsubishi* means). But since their product range is infinitely wide (ranging from aircraft to canned pears, from chicken food to transistors) and their position in Japan so all-pervading, one wonders whether it is a policy that is necessarily right, and whether it would suit other companies with diverse product ranges.

While there are reasons for closer integration of the visible manifestations of a large organization, they must be considered in relation to the market and product range. To assume, as people sometimes do, that all a firm needs is a common symbol is to resort to what one London designer calls 'the bailiff approach' – sticking a label on everything.

In fact, the communication problems of a group invariably mean reconciling numbers of conflicting and valid arguments, to arrive at a simplification that is not an excessively restricting or damaging strait jacket. Included must be a detailed consideration of any further situation that may arise.

International organizations face all of these problems, and more, but relatively few firms have coped with them really well. To the normal problems within the big company are added several structural ones which influence design and other communication policy. One of these is the incessant conflict between the local area and the international headquarters in attempting to arrive at a consistent impression. The man in France believes that things are different in France. He can point to different sales requirements – different outlets, competition, user habits, and the rest. Every country can do the same. Listen to them all and you're faced with anarchy. On the other hand it may be damaging to impose the same design on all countries.

A number of very large British companies have tended to the former policy (British American Tobacco, Hawker Siddeley, Reckitt & Colman, and others). Few consumers know that Odon Warland in Belgium is BAT; or that Brown & Williamson in the US is BAT; or that American Tobacco in Denmark is BAT; or Pioneer Tobacco in Ghana, or Nigerian Tobacco, or Malayan Tobacco, or others all over the world are BAT owned. Equally, many American companies have tended to the latter. Gillette, Ford, Kellogg, and Quaker are examples. Chrysler is a new one to add to the list.

The tendency is to increased international conformity, and the pattern of events may prove this to be right. But it needs qualifying. Some big companies fear nationalization – in their own country and in any other country where they are seen as important: the pattern is too familiar and is a brake to the activities of a number of companies. At the same time, the obviously foreign company runs the risk of suffering from local prejudice both against its success and against the country it comes from. This was one of the reasons why US Rubber changed its identity. Hot feelings about events in Vietnam and Little Rock led to demonstrations against the company in some Latin-American countries. They changed their name and deliberately chose a name both universal and usable anywhere – UniRoyal.

Even when the situation is less inflamed, more natural and friendly, the foreign company must always take particular action to integrate itself in the community and to be seen to be contributing to it. Often this is a question of communication – pointing out the problem to resident executives, shaping employee-relation policies, contributing time and effort to support local events, maintaining a particularly sensitive ear to the ground – establishing the company as a respected and welcome part of the community.

Even in the Western world's most sophisticated markets, care is needed. In the great developing markets, the problem is evident.

In fact, it is remarkable how few truly international organizations exist. Even within the Common Market, for example, the majority of companies are still in essence one-country firms with a percentage of exports to other

The Reversing Pyramid of Income. This chart, showing the changing disposition of wealth in the US, points to a basic shift in society. It suggests that many long-held attitudes must alter, and that communication to mass audiences must be considered in new terms.

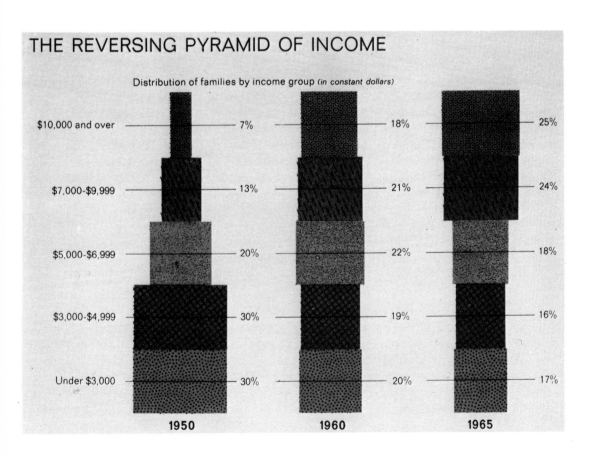

THE REVERSING PYRAMID OF INCOME

Distribution of families by income group *(in constant dollars)*

	1950	1960	1965
$10,000 and over	7%	18%	25%
$7,000-$9,999	13%	21%	24%
$5,000-$6,999	20%	22%	18%
$3,000-$4,999	30%	19%	16%
Under $3,000	30%	20%	17%

EEC countries. But not all exporters recognize that, even though they may be household names in their own country, they are unknown elsewhere. This relationship of company to market, alters the communication from it. If a company has different degrees of acceptance and recognition in various countries, its communication should vary accordingly.

The correct assessment of this problem would be to communicate in a manner most likely to evoke a good response from people in the country in relation to one's products. The basic reasons for purchasing goods are extremely important. We buy some things *because* they are imported. Peak Frean enjoyed great success in Canada because, even though the factory was there for all to see, people thought its biscuits were of imported quality: they were good. If Chanel were to make scent in Blackburn, Lancashire, perhaps English attitudes to the product would alter. Then again, other articles might *not* be bought simply because they were foreign.

There's a good deal of executive vanity in the global approach to design. The executive travels and likes to see his product and corporate name in every capital and on every shelf. And here is the key to an important distinction: some people travel a lot, most don't. Perhaps if one has products or services that are bought by the minority who travel, then they should be the same everywhere. Senior business executives, their wives and other well-off people may be among these. So, if one has consultancy services or products bought by middle and senior management – computers, chemical plant – then there is a strong case for one single worldwide identity. This is true of certain high-quality consumer products – whisky, certain brands of cigarette. In advertisements these would be pictured in polo clubs and in the lounges of the UN, and there's a certain glamorized truth about it.

Another category meriting serious thought of an international image is, of course, the excellent or unique. For Rolls-Royce, Dior, Dunhill, or Tiffany to change their names in other countries is wrong. More firms than justly warrant this claim, no doubt believe they merit it. An electrical appliance manufacturer once claimed, 'everyone in the world' knew his company. It took £30,000 and a year's research to prove the fact, obvious from sales figures, that this was not so.

Another class might be the companies who could benefit from their nation's image. Right or wrong, people think Americans good at electronic machines, for instance, but less good at producing wine. They think the opposite of Spain. They think Finns good at design, but that they would be less knowledgeable about reliability and service.

Such attitudes, deeply rooted as they are, can change. The changed attitude to Japanese cameras, and now motor cycles and cars, is proof of what can be accomplished. Resistance to purchase on nationalistic grounds is declining, but, nonetheless, these general attitudes may influence individual companies.

There are other possible considerations. Businessmen see the opportunity to cut promotion costs by using similar material everywhere. This may be right; but it may also mean that a great deal is inappropriate, and so wasted.

There are certain publications which are read internationally. If one is aiming at senior executives or a minority population it may be right to appear the same in all of them. But the truth is that most people do not travel very much, apart from occasional holidays when they purchase little. Thus, the endeavours made by certain soap and food manufacturers to standardize their packaging universally may be misconceived; if in so doing they make it less appropriate to a local market, by having to conform to an international or foreign standard, then any economies seem futile.

The problems of corporate communication become more complex when a company intends to operate internationally. Beware the facile global approach, while recognizing the growing need to simplify.

This chapter has looked at some of the problems involved in determining the basic communication goals of the organization. They are subtler than they seem. No serious design work should start until everyone is clear about the objectives.

Usually the design consultants appointed to consider these questions write a report, following their studies, in which they define the important areas to consider, and make recommendations for decision. This is a crucial stage, worthy of penetrating thought by the executives concerned and even by the most senior executive.

3

About people

Which ideas are capable of being communicated? Will people accept anything you say? Will certain people accept some ideas more readily than others? If they don't know the answer, designer and industry risk failure by trying to convey the unacceptable.

The person who communicates without studying the attitudes and way of life of those he wishes to influence, stands only a small chance of success. Regrettably, this is what has happened in the past. Only now are new attitudes, demanding deeper knowledge, gaining currency in industry. Understanding the fundamentals can help us know what ideas are capable of being transmitted, and which are unlikely to succeed.

The late James Brown, a Scottish psychiatrist who wrote several books on psychology and psychiatry, and became the deputy director of the Institute of Social Psychiatry in London, studied the use of propaganda. A Freudian psychologist, he believed that attitudes arise in one or more of these ways: (a) during the first five or six years of childhood; (b) by association with individuals and groups in later life; (c) as a result of unique or isolated experiences, or similar experiences undergone throughout life.

Dr Brown refers to a Law of Primacy which states that the earlier an experience the more potent its effect, since it influences the way later experiences will be interpreted. The direct relevance of this study of attitude formation, and particularly of childhood, becomes obvious, too, when we consider international communications.

Are people all the same? Will they respond equally to the same global messages? According to Dr Brown:

It is a waste of time to attempt facile interpretations of behaviour in terms of a universal human nature based upon fixed instinct which will respond uniformly to the same appeals. [He claims, also, that] Complex as modern countries are, each instils or attempts to instil particular attitudes in its inhabitants . . . , in spite of the complexity of their social structure, Spaniards, Germans, French, Japanese and Englishmen do tend to differ in quite significant ways which are important in understanding their responses. . . . These differences have nothing to do with physical factors of race or heredity. On the contrary, they are attitudes learned from childhood onwards but primarily based on child-rearing patterns which in turn are presumably related to the peoples' geographical situation, history and traditions. They form the overall design which family and social groups employ when they are unconsciously moulding the individual character, that is to say, attitude.

According to Melanie Klein, whose work with children is widely accepted, two emotions arise in the very earliest stages of development which remain persistent throughout life. They have great relevance to later responses. These are anxiety and guilt. The theory of this need not concern us here except for two conclusions. First, it appears that the way infants react to these stresses helps influence whether they tend towards authoritarianism or humanitarianism in later life; whether their conscience is based largely on fear of punishment or fear of disappointing their loved ones. Second, although this is primarily the realm of the propagandist, there is no doubt that in some cases industry finds that its products are preferred by people in one group rather than the other.

This basic trait forms a central point of what psychologists call 'the nuclear personality'. Around the centre cluster other attitudes as time goes by, which tend to be all of a piece. People may argue whether it is morally acceptable for industry to know so much about its customers and to exploit their knowledge, but it is done. Any number of advertisements appeal to this primary anxiety or guilt, this basic authoritarian or humanitarian attitude in people.

It is a basic tenet that the 'nuclear personality' created in these first few years is both deeply rooted and highly resistant to change. Put bluntly, it seems you can trade on it, but not alter it. If this is so, one can see why manufacturers want to know more. It could be that at least some of their promotion *and image creation* attempts are certain to fail because they are directed unwittingly at the wrong people, or aim to change attitudes not susceptible to change.

Melanie Klein argues that during a child's first five or six years there are three stages of learning: *orally*, when a need for love and protection is established; *anally*, when importance of time and regularity is learnt, including learning that it is possible to be controlled by and to control others (already one sees sharp differences between national behaviour; cleanliness, order, and obedience appear related); and *Oedipus* or *Electra*. In this last stage the child learns by watching others (mother or father) and acquires attitudes to authority: what works for the child now tends to become habitual. It is from here, according to Miss Klein, that much of our later life is controlled – when we go on learning by watching others. This echoes Professor David Riesman's view that in mass society behaviour is increasingly controlled by the behaviour of others.

Again, one can see a direct relevance between this statement and the decisions a company makes about its communication strategy. The next thought brings it into still sharper focus.

Following childhood, people come into contact with others outside the home. But society is not the homogeneous mass we sometimes think. It is composed of groups of people either deliberately organized (church, work, politics, unions), or informally coming together (family, friends, gangs of adolescents, school groups). It is now thought that people get their satisfactions and standards from such groups.

An Australian psychologist, Elton Mayo, once showed how these groups operate in a factory. He claimed that management must recognize and relate itself to the informal group rather than to individuals. He wrote:

> In every department . . . the workers have – whether aware of it or not – formed themselves into groups with appropriate customs, duties, routines, even rituals; and management succeeds (or fails) in proportion as it is accepted without reservation by these as author and leader.

It is important to realize that people absorb some of their standards from the groups they belong to. And these standards are what the psychologists would call 'peripheral'. They are not necessarily deeply rooted. They can be changed. The length of time one has held a 'peripheral' opinion may be important. A young man will switch brands of cigarette without a thought. An old man may be extremely put out if the tobacco he has smoked for fifty years is not to be found. A young housewife may find difficulty in switching from a brand of gravy browning her mother swore by.

But the problem gets more involved because individuals often belong to a number of groups that adhere to different standards. This is another consequence of our modern, explosive, free society. People in static situations, rooted in their local communities, feel few of the cross-currents that affect the modern, politically aware, socially ambitious commuter and parent.

Perhaps the mass media tend to homogenize people and attitudes; yet still the farmer remains a long way from the clerk. But the dilemma doesn't lie in these extremes. Rather, it lies in the lives of the very people who, increasing urbanization has shown us, form the new mass markets. Finding the groups from which a customer takes the standards appropriate to your industry is a specific task for researchers.

Even without seeking out such groups, the modern manager should be aware that an increasingly large part of his audience suffers from these counter-stresses. In his 'family group', a man should take the kids to the park on Saturday; but on Monday his work colleagues will ask him if he saw the football match. During the week his wife will want him to be home early to help prepare for guests; but his boss may ask him to stay at work, or his photographic club meets that night. The local amenities committee he sits on is mostly conservative; the union he belongs to is anything but. Success in any dimension, invariably involving extra commitment, increases the stresses in others.

As we saw earlier, management should recognize the modern situation and act in such a way as to benefit from it. It should be seen as both an opportunity and obligation to ease such tensions. In advertising one has seen attempts made to reconcile contradictory group pressures. So-called 'prestige' promotion that shows how the good of the firm benefits society, or particular sections of it, can be seen as such an attempt. This suggests that, rather than eliminate all promotion that is not specifically related to product sales, one should reshape it and increase it.

Dr Brown distinguishes between *character traits*, which are extremely resistant to change; *attitudes*, which, tending to reflect the group, can be of fairly long standing, and *opinions*, which can be readily changed. Of attitudes, he says that these are often based on character traits. From a flood of stimuli, the person tends to select those most consistent with his deep beliefs.[1]

Other studies show that each item of a person's attitude is correlated. The deeper they lie the harder they are to change, and to change piecemeal.

It is significant that sophisticated advertisers try to tie their company or product to motivations that lie deeper than the superficial opinion level. But examples exist of organizations that have squandered millions trying to change attitudes that are too firmly rooted to alter.

The late Ed Murrow, speaking of the power of TV, said, 'It can retard or accelerate a trend in public opinion, but never reverse it.'

Industry would be well advised to find out whether its aspirations and claims are in line with what is acceptable to its specific audiences. Designers and image-makers, too, would be wise to satisfy themselves that the communication goals they define are appropriate in this context to their client's audiences.

Further, the audience should be addressed in the right way. It is thought that the 'peripheral attitudes', which appear to the layman to be the level one might optimistically aim at, are a function of the *group* rather than of the isolated individual, and can only be changed by altering the group attitude collectively. Research also suggests that to try to alter an individual's attitudes by direct instruction is to imply that he is wrong; it is an axiom, according to G W Allport,[2] that, 'people cannot be taught who feel they are, at the same time, being attacked'.

Freud described how attitudes of groups or individuals may be developed.

All are a response to frustration, which leads to a desire to change attitude. Among them are: *rationalization*; *displacement*, in which the thwarted goal is replaced by a substitute; *projection*, in which the impulses people do not want to see in themselves are attributed to others (group solidarity is often achieved by projecting all wickedness against another group); *identification*, the success of group leaders is partly related to their ability to act as a substitute for the person, usually the parent, with whom the individual first learnt to identify; *compensation*, when the original goal is frustrated, another goal is sought through a drive which has not been involved in the original frustration; *conformity*, the desire to be like other people.

The reader will forgive such a cursory glance at topics worth deeper study. Here, our attempt is only to suggest that if these are ways in which attitudes may be altered the reader will wish his attention drawn to them, and indeed to other schools of thought.

The Russian physiologist and contemporary of Freud, I P Pavlov, whose experiments with dogs (in 1901) are well known, made important discoveries regarding patterns of behaviour. Of considerable interest in medicine, they seem beyond the interest of this book, as are the use of hypnotism, drugs, and newer methods attempted to alter attitudes. James Vicary's theories of subliminal perception enjoyed a brief vogue a few years ago. The ideas were not especially new: Aristotle spoke of the possibility, Leibniz wrote about it, while Jung, Ohm, Dixon, and others worked on it. Vicary himself admitted that his methods were not particularly effective.

Ideas of communication that may have relevance to our subject were expounded in a book written by Californian psychiatrist Eric Berne. It was in the *New York Times* best-seller list for over two years and called *Games People Play*,[3] it claimed that each individual has three 'ego states' – the parental, adult, and child ego state. It then claimed that in all their contacts people find themselves in one or other of these positions. The three states imply: (a) that every individual carries within him a 'set of ego states that reproduce those of his parents (as he perceived them)'; (b) that every individual is capable of objective data processing if the appropriate ego state can be achieved; (c) that every individual carries within him 'fixated relics' from earlier years that can be activated. According to Dr Berne, we exhibit all three layers at various times.

He says the parent is exhibited in two forms. First, directly: the person responds as his own father or mother actually responded. Second, indirectly: he responds the way they wanted him to. In the first place, he becomes one of them; in the second, he adapts himself to their requirements. This parental state has two functions: it enables the individual to act effectively as a parent of actual children, and it makes many responses automatic. Many things are done because 'that's the way it's done'.

The child is also exhibited in two forms, claims Dr Berne. The *adapted* child modifies his behaviour under parental influence. He behaves as his parents want him to, or he withdraws and whines. The *natural* child, he says, is spontaneous. He may be rebellious or creative. Intuition, creativity, spontaneous drive, and enjoyment reside here. If you think of intoxication, this is made clear. Dr Berne says:

> Visually this decommissions the parent, so the adapted child is free from parental influence, and is transformed by release into the natural child.

The *adult* is necessary for survival. It computes the probabilities in everyday life (works out if it is safe to cross roads). It also mediates between parent and child.

Now the significance of this is that when we communicate with others we speak from one of these states. Satisfactory relations continue only as long as the response is complementary. If you speak as an adult and the reply is given as an adult, that's fine. The fevered child asks for water and the mother brings it (child to parent). If you speak as a parent, and the person responds as a child, that is complementary, and relations proceed. To quote Dr Berne again:

> As long as the transactions are complementary it is irrelevant whether two people are engaging in critical gossip (parent–parent), solving a problem (adult–adult) or playing together (child–child).

Communication breaks off, however, when a cross-transaction occurs. The most common in marriage, love, work, and friendship, is when a dialogue starts as adult to adult, and is responded to differently. An example Dr Berne quotes is this:

> 'Do you know where my cuff links are?' The appropriate adult response might be 'on the desk'. But the 'child' response might be: 'you blame me for everything'; or the parent response might be 'why don't you look after your things, you're not a child any more'.

Communication breaks off at that point until people start making complementary responses again. In this example, the man who mislaid his cufflinks could reply as a child, or as a parent, and establish communication again.

At first sight, all this seems unrelated to corporate communications. But is it? How many strikes occur because bosses behave as parents to children when they should speak as adult to adult? Or when addressed as adults, unions reply as children? Or when unions speaking as adults, are reprimanded as children? How many advertisements succeed because they speak the right way, and how many fail because their efforts are wrongly directed? A moment's thought shows that there are many situations in business life, and many in the mass communications process, where Dr Berne's theories become sharply relevant. One wonders whether a good deal of employee-relations effort is rendered useless and even damaging because it inevitably evokes the wrong response. How much advertising fails because it is wrongly positioned: (parental when it requires an adult response, or adult when it needs a parental response)?

An advertising campaign was launched in West Germany in 1967 by the Dresdner Bank. Among the ads were some which pointed out that a new system the bank had developed enabled people to budget their savings, and so plan to be sure of protecting and educating their children. It required, we might say, both an adult response (to analyse the budget system) and a protective, parental one (to want to do what is necessary to care for one's children). The double-page advertisements showed a full colour page and a half photograph of a young child looking up at the reader. Was this a 'child' to 'parent' appeal? The remaining space described and showed the budget system. Was this an adult-to-adult transaction? The campaign set Germany talking and was, according to the bank, a remarkable success.

It might be stimulating to mix our theories. First, notice that the campaign appeared in West Germany which is said to be, relatively speaking, an authoritarian, disciplined, but not unsentimental, society. To appeal to a German audience as child to parent, and to urge the discipline of regular saving, may both be fruitful approaches. It is conceivable, too, that such approaches may be more successful there than in some other countries. Once more the need to think of countries specifically, to appeal to each in its own terms, is underlined.

To take this one step further, it is interesting to wonder whether, within West Germany, the Dresdner Bank advertisements tended to appeal more to one type of person than another. We saw earlier a basic division of people into authoritarian (respect for discipline, fear of punishment) and humanitarian (fear of disappointing or hurting loved ones). If research were able to demonstrate any weighting, one way or the other, this might be of considerable importance to the bank's future promotion and image projection.

Talking on a broader theme, designer Evert Endt in Paris once said, 'Research techniques aren't available to give us the information we want.' It may be that this kind of information cannot be gathered either. But such knowledge, if attainable, could have a significant effect on our approach to corporate communications.

With such knowledge a company could (a) tailor its products or services to be more precisely what its actual potential customers require, (b) relate its promotion more accurately to its audiences and its products, (c) shape its corporate image and communications to appeal to its actual potential audience, and (d) eliminate 'waste circulation', and appeal to other audiences (in this context) in different ways. The result would be more effective and more economical communications.

Dr Berne's ideas go further, and into more detail than is relevant to our purpose. There are, however, other comments which should be mentioned to understand his concept. One is that the parent protects the child most until each social situation has been tested. Another is that these transactions can work at two levels. Beneath the overt, *social* level, may lie a *psychological* or *ulterior* level of response. And these two levels can go on at the same time.

This is one view of the kind of conversation that appears to be about one thing but is, in fact, about another.

Dr Berne cites two examples. The salesman says, 'This product is better but it really costs more than you can afford.' It sounds adult to adult, but is adult to child. If the housewife thinks, 'I'll show him I'm as good as any of his customers', she is responding as a child. The transaction is therefore complementary. She buys, appearing to move as an adult.

Any sales dialogue illustrates that all levels are possible in one conversation: parent–parent, adult–adult, child–child, their complementary combination, and (switching in and out as the conversation goes on) the ulterior level.

Or, because it is irresistible, take the conversation of the cowboy who says to the visitor, 'Let me show you the barn.' It sounds adult–adult; psychologically it's something else. She replies, 'I've loved barns since I was a girl,' (she's understood his ulterior 'child–child' message and replied in his 'adult–adult' way).

Dr Berne believes that transactions are not random, but programmed into sequences designed to manipulate reality. All societies have their greeting rituals, ranging from the casual 'hi' in the US to long, oriental versions. They become stereotyped, predictable, and expected. Even the balance of these 'rituals' is neatly, though intuitively, judged. Furthermore, it is necessary to respect them. If inadvertently one upsets the balance, by excess or neglect, communications can suffer.

This suggests that in our communications to any audience (the trade, Press, employees, suppliers, and customers) we should observe the rituals already established. To be suddenly friendly, and to jump abruptly to new levels of intimacy without honouring the protocol, as it were, can cause anxiety. Indeed, one sees people put on the defensive (and thus inhibiting communication) by advertising which assumes a level of contact before it is willingly given. If it can be true in long-distance communication, it is doubly so in direct human relations. The contacts of executives with their staff, PR men with the Press, salesmen with the trade are all better for being considered in this way.

This, too, has international implications. We've said that the rituals normal and expected in the US are different from those in Japan. All societies have built their rituals and though they may be altering swiftly, in favour of the faster, more direct and informal American approach, they are to be respected. Companies from one country have failed in another because they neglected this homily. For example, in England businessmen switch to Christian names only slightly less quickly than in the US. In Germany, where there is tremendous respect for professional titles, formal relationships, and a strict 'pecking order', Christian names are used reluctantly. From France to Norway the change of relationship is subject to a formal exchange. Curiously, though, double standards exist. A German, Norwegian, or Frenchman may well be on Christian-name terms with an American he hardly knows, and on more formal surname terms with people he works with every day.

The importance of understanding the established codes of conduct is relevant. The effectiveness of one's communication in other countries is influenced by the extent to which one appreciates the prevailing social structure and attitudes.

It is still rare to see companies using this knowledge as an instrument of policy in communication. You see firms in formal, perhaps authoritarian, industries behaving formally and projecting themselves formally. Others, in more haphazard, relaxed occupations project themselves that way. But mostly this happens as Alexander Plunket Greene said of the firm of Mary Quant, 'Our image happens because of the people we are.' There is a rough appropriateness about it all which works most of the time, but it is easy to picture situations in which it all goes wrong. An American bank may fail in Germany if it projects itself in the same open, friendly, and eager way that is suitable at home. A French dress designer may be misunderstood if he sets up a distinguished and discreet boutique in extrovert, permissive Carnaby Street. If people want creativity above all from an advertising agency they may reject creative directors who have the formality of brokers on the Stock Exchange.

This can be expanded if one thinks of the authoritarian and permissive analogy in educational terms. It has been argued that people who are better educated, subject to 'parental' (including teacher) authority longer, tend to respect rational, intellectual behaviour. They try to control their feelings. ('A gentleman is only rude intentionally.') The broad, middle band of people also control their emotions most of the time, but occasionally give vent to them and, indeed, believe that such release is desirable ('a little of what you fancy does you good'). People less subject to 'parental' control, less educated, may act more impulsively.

When communist Jack Dash brought London's huge docks to a standstill for weeks, the chairman of the Dock Board issued formal statements of regret couched in terms unlikely to alienate anyone. The broad mass of Britons made it fully clear that they were annoyed, but did nothing: a docker's wife punched Jack Dash on the nose.

The communication implications are clear. It is possible to hypothesize that designs aimed at the top strata may be more formal, logical, intellectual, restrained. Design aimed at mass markets might be less structured and show varying degrees of permissiveness, colourfulness, excitement. It is noteworthy that the strict, austere disciplines of the Bauhaus which still affect European design, sprang from an intellectual élite in Germany keen to impose order on an anarchic situation.

In a state of flux, Western society is not certain whether to be more permissive or more puritan. Demonstrating both to excess, it totters between the two. The levelling up and levelling down of incomes and social behaviour also confuse the once clearly stratified picture; as does the new, sharp division in the UK and Western Europe between generations.

An example of the effect socio-economic strata may have on corporate communications was illustrated by a study carried out in 1959 by Robert S Lee, then a communications research psychologist at IBM. The company wished to study its corporate image and to probe public attitudes to automation. The reason for doing so indicates why this is such a well-thought-of and distinguished organization. It has a direct bearing on all companies who see themselves as progressive, and want to be known as such.

In the next ten years there will be more technological strides and more automation. Industry will be more efficient, better informed, better able to control widespread activities. But personnel needs will change, and automated equipment in factories may put people out of work. Obviously many new problems are created. (About such machines, a Ford executive once said to Union boss Walter Reuther, 'You're going to have a tough time getting them to join the Union,' Reuther replied, 'And you're going to find it hard selling them cars.') For good reason feelings can run high on this subject. IBM appreciate that public attitudes about automation can have an influence on the company's image quite independent of the acts of the company, its public relations programme, or even of the real consequences of the issue. And that is why, said Mr Lee,

> . . . such a corporation must have timely and appropriate intelligence on its public relations environment. IBM therefore began to research the state of public opinion towards automation and to relate this to the Company's current and potential corporate image.

They found, as one might expect, that familiarity with the term 'automation' is strongly related to educational level. Over 80 per cent of the people in the sample who had completed college had heard of automation. The figure dropped to 62 per cent for people who had completed high school. Only 20 per cent of people who had not been to high school had ever heard the word 'automation'. Mr Lee is quick to point out that the level of formal education is not the only factor influencing whether or not an individual has heard of automation. IBM studied people by their level of 'cultural sophistication', whatever their formal education. (A person high in cultural sophistication would prefer classical to pop music, appreciate art and literature, value knowledge that has no immediate practical use. . . .) Familiarity with the subject of automation was much greater among the more sophisticated, regardless of formal schooling. They found the same with current affairs. People interested in current affairs tend to be familiar with automation. People not interested in current affairs tend to be less familiar with automation. And it was the same with people interested in mechanics.

Put them together and you find that 91 per cent of male high school graduates who are culturally sophisticated, interested in current affairs, and mechanically curious, have heard about automation. At the other end of the scale: of women who did not complete high school, who are culturally unsophisticated, interested neither in current affairs nor in mechanics, only 13 per cent had heard of automation.

IBM sees everything from products to buildings as an expression of the corporation. Quality is achieved by using outstanding designers and architects. Pictures show: (a) IBM System 360 designed by Eliot Noyes; (b) a detail of the IBM laboratory near Nice by Marcel Breuer; (c) their laboratory outside New York by Paul Randolph; (d) a plant in Minnesota by Eero Saarinen.

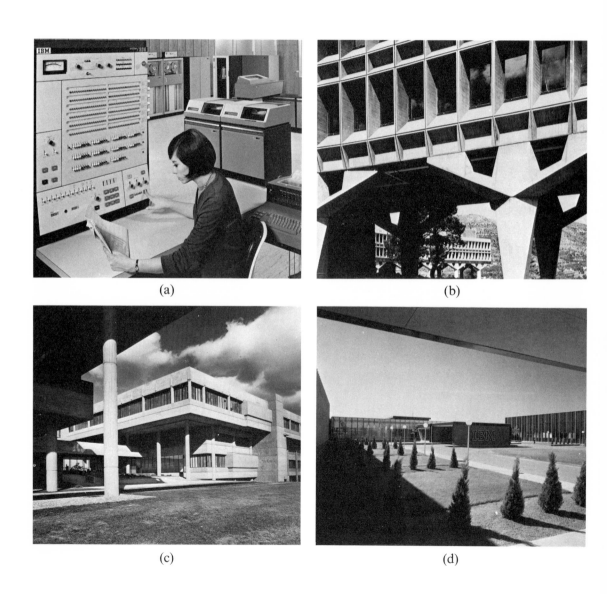

(a)

(b)

(c)

(d)

IBM took comfort from this. The people who knew about automation were the best equipped to 'understand its importance to the economy'. When they penetrated further, IBM found two major 'belief systems' about automation: one they called the *progress* image, the other the *dangers* image.

The ideas are really self-evident. *Progress:* automation will bring a higher standard of living, more leisure, more comforts. Life will become easier and more interesting. *Dangers:* mainly concerned with the fear that automation will cause unemployment; older people and smaller businesses will have a tough time.

A lot of people see both sides. Half the people who think automation will raise living standards, also thought it will create unemployment. 35 per cent say automation is a good thing; 4 per cent say it is a bad thing; 66 per cent agree with the 'progress' image; 54 per cent agree with the 'dangers' image; 76 per cent say automation will raise the standard of living; and 51 per cent think it will create a lot of unemployment.

IBM asked why it is that some people feel one way, some another. What social and psychological factors encourage or facilitate adherence to the 'progress' belief system, for example? They found that education and cultural sophistication didn't have much to do with it, but socio-economic position did. The findings suggest that people who are financially secure are more likely to see automation as a progressive development.

Optimism about the future is also an important factor. Still more important is an 'open-minded and generally receptive attitude towards the new and different'. Belief in the good aspects of automation (the 'progress' image):

> . . . is exceptionally strong among those open-minded people who have a curiosity about mechanical things and who are optimistic about the future of the economy.

There is an entirely different pattern for the 'dangers' image. Those who are most worried are the people who are pessimistic about the future of the economy, and often the poorer, less well educated.

IBM uncovered a syndrome of ideas that makes some people apprehensive and anxious about uncertainties in a swiftly changing world. (They tend to be anti-intellectual, suspicious of science, wanting more government control over business, and simpler and more direct solutions from strong leadership.) When you couple this apprehension with pessimism about the future of the economy, concern about the dangers of automation becomes extreme.

What this study shows us is that, although socio-economic factors influence attitudes, underlying psychological factors are still more telling.

IBM next related itself to these attitudes. It felt able to measure what people think of its 'corporate citizenship' treatment of employees, calibre of management, importance of IBM's growth, and products to national welfare, it's scientific and technical capabilities, and the degree to which it is seen as unfair and domineering in its methods.

Among the findings was a surprising one: association of the company with automation increases its scientific prestige regardless of whether people welcome or fear automation. They learnt that in the US many people are optimistic about the future. They look forward to a better world as a result of further progress in science and technology. But there are fears.

Speculating about the future, Robert Lee said to a congress in New York:

we might infer that any forces or events that would increase this apprehension may also raise fears about changing technology. These forces do not necessarily have to be economic in nature, but could include various other challenges to social and psychological adaptation, such as living with the threat of a world holocaust, rapid changes in moral standards, or shifts in the power and status of groups previously considered inferior.

One fascinating aspect of this study is that it shows how people can hold apparently contradictory beliefs at the same time. Technological progress is good because it will bring a better world. It is bad because it will also change things, and upset employment unless handled carefully. A conclusion might be that to stress the benefits and glamour of a situation may do little to decrease the fear of it. Again, one is drawn to the view that any organization must make its communication goals practical. It must recognize where it can hope to influence attitudes and where it cannot. How much one can guess about this, without benefit of research, is questionable.

Another important lesson from the IBM study is the degree of probing and analysis that is possible. The care taken (far greater than our brief résumé shows) to shred evidence and shred again in order to learn is impressive. The first finding (that knowledge of automation is related to education) is not taken at face value, and in the end, was found not to be, by any means, the most significant.

Underlying psychological factors are highly important to effective communication.

An amusing example of how superficial understanding can backfire occurred early in the Second World War. During the so-called 'phony war', French troops from the south manned the Maginot line. German loudspeakers told them that the English had landed in the north and were already making love to Frenchwomen. The soldiers laughed. Their wives and girl friends were safe in the south, and local patriotism put the north beyond their interest.

This chapter has been about some of the people with whom the modern corporation is trying to communicate. Not a complete study, it is intended to suggest that a deeper understanding of human motivations and attitudes can have a marked bearing on the effectiveness of corporate communications. One has seen a number of ideas that, if valid, cast doubt on a lot of the corporate identity work often seen and applauded. If it opens the way to a higher standard of performance in real terms by widening the criteria by which design and other communication activity are judged, it will be worth while.

A number of the explanations of human behaviour give practical guides to action. Not least is recognition of the influence of the small group (from which the 'teach-in' has grown). Experiments have shown that where lectures fail to change attitudes, letting people discuss a problem among themselves with a skilled person present with any facts that are needed, yields good results. The facts have become *their* facts, the decision to change, *theirs*. We have seen the power of the small group in influencing the attitudes most susceptible to change by any medium.

Confirmed from several points of view has been the need to think 'local'. In this age of international business and global communications, it is something to remember. Despite the natural wish and all the commercial pressure to present the company uniformly everywhere, there is ample evidence that it is unwise to leap to automatic or doctrinal decisions. Situations are always specific and must be thought through with care.

REFERENCES

1. *Techniques of Persuasion* (Pelican A604), Penguin, 1963.
2. *The Nature of Prejudice*, Doubleday, 1950.
3. Deutsch, 1966.

How to set about a corporate identity programme

We have established the need to consider corporate communications, and have touched on a number of things to think about. In this chapter we will ask how to go about it, basing comments as far as possible on the practical experience of others.

Once more it is necessary to stress that each situation is particular. While general attitudes prevail, it is dangerous to seek facile solutions. Every successful corporate identity is a specific answer to a particular set of marketing, political, and human situations.

The first and fundamental requirement of every successful corporate identity programme is that it is treated seriously. One of the most outstanding design programmes of this kind in the world is IBM's. Using only the best architects, and the best graphic and product designers, IBM has unquestionably enhanced its world reputation. There is no doubt that a reason for the quality and effectiveness of this project has been the close personal involvement of the company president, Tom Watson, no less than the calibre of designers he retains. In 1966, Mr Watson received the Tiffany Award which is given for the encouragement of American design. Presenting the award, Tiffany's chairman said:

It is the chief executive who . . . initiates this kind of thing, who handles it with understanding, encourages his designers, procures the kind of designer that he needs for his particular business and then brings it to fruition. [He continued] There are many, many designers who are frustrated

les professionnels
des hommes qui font confiance à Firestone

ce pilote pose 91,6 tonnes sur la piste d'atterrissage

Au même instant 91,6 tonnes écrasent impitoyablement
les pneumatiques. Ces pneus subissent – en une fraction de seconde –
une fantastique accélération: 0-265 km/h... sans transition.

Cet effort extraordinaire exige des pneus qui satisfont aux normes
de sécurité les plus élevées. En tant que professionnels, les pilotes du
monde entier font quotidiennement confiance à Firestone.

Firestone construit des pneus pour
les conditions d'utilisation les plus extrêmes.
On peut faire confiance à l'expérience des
ingénieurs Firestone.

C'est pourquoi des millions d'automobilistes
roulent sur Firestone.

Firestone
performances et sécurité

Comparison: two tyre companies project themselves differently. Firestone, inspiring the confidence of professionalism (though with an oddly inappropriate Gothic logo-type) seriously concentrates on the decisive moment. Pirelli expresses confidence, too, but light-heartedly. The Pirelli advertisement, by André François, shows that even the biggest companies can relax, and logotypes can be played with without loss of respect or recognition.

because the boss doesn't seem, number one, to have a plan; and number two, he may . . . start and he may stop and nothing may happen . . . and these talented people, these designers, can't work under these conditions. This is not what Tom Watson did at IBM. He decided to start this programme. He procured very good talent in the various fields . . . in architecture, product designing and in various other fields of design . . . and he initiated the programme with them, worked it out, helped them so that their job could be done properly and easily and economically and out came this remarkable job.

Designers with experience of corporate identity will always tell you that the chairman or managing director is the right man to put the weight of his office, and his enthusiasm, behind any such work. Sainsburys, the British supermarket chain, has already been mentioned as outstanding in its design policies. Peter Dixon, the design chief responsible, has direct access to Lord Sainsbury and his son and 'may see him fifteen times a day'.

Preparing this book the author asked a famous designer what were the main reasons for success or failure in this work. Instantly he replied: 'Unless the top man endorses the design policy it is a waste of money.' It is true that a number of good schemes have been created and directed by others, but frequently this involves decision by stealth and even subterfuge. Results may come in the end, but there is always the risk that good schemes will die for the wrong reasons. The marketing director and group PRO share with the chief executive freedom to move over large areas of the organization. And this is essential. Corporate identity work at best involves the whole organization. Occasionally a group endeavour has started in one section of the organization, and spread to the whole. This is much more a tribute to the political expertise of the executive handling it than anything else.

Enthusiasm and real support by the chief executive is virtually indispensable. One sad case history will illustrate this. A big and famous British company once started to develop a corporate identity programme. The PRO, reporting to the vice-chairman, interviewed a number of leading design organizations and appointed one of them. Thorough briefing took place. Design work was submitted and approved by the vice-chairman and then by the chairman and his board. It then went to the deputy chairman's committee on which sat thirty managing directors of companies in the group. Twenty-eight approved, two disapproved. To satisfy those two, the whole exercise was repeated, with new designs, but with identical results.

Each time the chairman gave his approval, but not his support. In the end the whole scheme foundered on the sectional interests of two subordinates.

It is the reality of large organizations that there will always be opponents; always be some who risk losing in the general gain. To effect anything as far-reaching or all-pervasive as a change of corporate identity one must be ready to meet and resolve sectional interests. This often means arbitrating, sometimes means overruling. Here is an evident case for senior involvement and drive.

Another illustration of this occurred in 1965 when the marketing director of a well-known electrical appliance manufacturer instituted an image programme. After all the intermediate acceptances, the design scheme was shown to a board of nine men. The managing director, marketing director, and others approved it. One objected. The whole exercise was slowed down and dead within six months. Here again was a failure by the chairman to support and drive through a scheme that needed his weight.

The need for the chairman's support can be seen in other ways. After due research and design effort, the managing director, marketing director, and others in a large shipbuilding company approved the rapid full-scale application of a new corporate identity. The chairman, to whom the scheme was shown, then so decimated the concept that changing the letterhead slightly became a victory for the management.

Sometimes months or years of painstaking corporate identity planning is treated as a political ping-pong ball at board meetings. If the most senior executive identifies himself with the corporate communication policy, there is less chance of this happening.

To a lesser extent, the same applies to money. Sometimes these programmes fail because, while the board approves the principles, departmental managers are reluctant to spend the money involved. The board of a company must recognize that abnormal expenditures will be necessary. The money needed may come from existing budgets, no doubt, but not totally. The board can remove an inevitable source of irritation by making it clear that existing budgets will not be expected to stretch too far, and that the management will be given extra funds to carry out this work.

This attitude to money is another aspect of the prime requirement: to treat corporate identity work seriously.

A well-executed corporate identity policy will have important long-term effects; it does a good deal to influence the shape and position of the organization. As such, it *merits* the time of senior management, and *merits* this big approach.

Some companies belittle this work on the grounds that its value is imprecise and hard to measure. This is illogical. First, it fails to recognize the role of the modern corporation. Second, at a minimum level, every company values its goodwill and manages to put a figure for it in the balance sheet.

The president of the Chrysler Corporation defined the importance of this work to his company (he is spending an estimated $10 million on Chrysler's new corporate identity) when he said:

> Customers buy more than a product. The pressures of a free, competitive marketplace coupled with our country's extremely rapid technological development, have generated a situation in which the customer tends to 'buy' the company that makes the product. They 'buy' its character, its

size, its sincerity, the confidence it inspires. Thus the function of our corporate identity system is to influence constructively the image of Chrysler as a corporation.

Don Burnham is the president of Westinghouse, a company with an extraordinarily wide range of products spread through seventy divisions. In 1967 he opened a new Design Centre to coordinate every visible manifestation of Westinghouse, from products to architecture, interior design to signing and graphics. At that time he said:

> We regard good design as a hard dollars-and-cents proposition . . . good design makes our products look better, work better, sell better. [He also said:] Good design is not something you do once and then figure it is done forever. I believe it is a continuing function, something like manufacturing and, in a growing company, it is happening every day.

Supposing the organization gets this far: deciding something needs to be done, and resolving to treat the matter earnestly. What happens next?

The next task must be to decide how to handle the project. The first step is to appoint an executive with special responsibility to the board – this may be the managing director, the marketing director, or the group PRO. In Tube Investments, the group PR director has been responsible to the chairman for skilfully building a groupwide coordinated design policy. In a situation where seventy companies are involved, the chairman's authority and support has been needed on several occasions. It has always been given.

An independent design consultant in London, is currently handling a total design programme for the John Lewis Partnership, a large chain of 21 department stores and 35 supermarkets. Even in this extremely democratic organization, where the 32,000 employees are partners in the business, much tribute is given to the strength of the chairman. He has set up a design committee which, with 22 members, may be too large for other organizations.

British Motor Holdings handled their programme in two phases. To get the job going, the company secretary took responsibility. He had the ear of the chairman and the authority to cut through almost any problems. When the design scheme was accepted by the board, he handed over responsibility to a committee of three who were to work with the consultants. He gave them a clear job description. That committee reported to the director of marketing on the main board. (The scheme got nowhere because the company merged with Leyland, who had different ideas.)

Milner Gray, who has been the principal of a design partnership in London since 1934, is emphatic about the need for clear organization. Whenever he starts working with a new client on a major design exercise, he aims to set up a two-part organization as he did when he rejuvenated the visual identity of British Rail. The first step is a working party. This, in the case of the railways, consisted of various interested department heads in the organization. The working party determined the work that needed to be done, reviewed the implications of it in the railways, and established recommendations. It took the work to the point of main presentation to the board.

When the board approved the main design proposals, that committee disbanded and another was formed. This, called a 'steering committee', has a railway executive as chairman. It has the task of seeing the whole approved programme through.

John Tandy, who also runs a London design office, advocates a similar policy. He thinks that, at the start, the chairman, managing director, or marketing director should be responsible, then later a coordinator should be appointed. But, he insists, this man should coordinate and not be assumed to be an expert on design.

The Chrysler Corporation set up a special 'corporate identity' office to follow through its design programme. The head of this office reports to the vice-president (administration).

General Mills in Minneapolis has appointed a 'co-ordinator of corporate identification'. He is the manager of creative services.

In 1965 Ford established a corporate identity office to:

. . . develop programmes and activities designed to improve our company's visual image in all areas of public exposure. [Their aim:] . . . to ensure that the company presents on a world wide basis a unified, attractive and readily recognizable appearance in all of its visual manifestations.

It may be unnecessary to set up a definitive organization at the start of a project. One can simply emerge. Indeed, there is much to be said for British Rail or British Motor Holdings two-stage structure. But a clear responsibility must be vested in someone – delegated or not – right from the start.

His first job must be to establish a basic brief and to appoint designers. Providing good designers are appointed, this first brief need be little more than a statement of intention, or a statement of the objective to be accomplished. The briefest directive of this kind ever given was to a designer, by Frederick Hooper, at that time managing director of Schweppes: 'We want to be known as the Rolls-Royce of soft drinks. Get on with it.'

The initial statement needs to be clear enough for the designers to prepare a plan and a work method, remembering that they will later want to gather detailed facts for themselves. Therefore, the model statement of intention might give very briefly: the name of the organization, its activities, organization, and markets, and a statement of the objective to be accomplished. Special factors should be referred to. For example, if it is thought important for the programme to be ready at a certain time, perhaps to coincide with a new product launch, a centenary, or a trade event, this certainly influences the planning from the designer's viewpoint and should be mentioned.

The importance of this early statement, and subsequent ones, was emphasized by Boston designer Joseph Selame when he said, 'Before you expect the public to know you, you must first know yourself.' Should this prove a stumbling-block, Mr Selame has pointed out 'the need to explain yourself to an outside consultant actually consolidates this self-knowledge . . .'.

This first document should be written succinctly and carefully; attitudes taken at that early stage may influence subsequent action. It should be given to the design group selected, or to the groups on a short list.

Designers should be invited to prepare a specific work plan to accomplish the objective, showing how they intend to isolate all the problems, and how they will present their creative solutions. They should give estimates of time and fees, and indicate how the follow-through would be handled. This last point is of great importance. In any corporate identity project there are at least three important stages: first, understanding the problem; second, creating good solutions; third, implementing them thoroughly. Examples abound of schemes that fail on all three points. If they do fail, each is a waste of time, money, and opportunity, though none worse than the last.

An English designer with experience in this field, believes 'the quality and consistency of application is very important', and there are few who would disagree. Not only is this true in terms of effectiveness, but also of economy. To apply a design scheme to all the types of paper, all vehicles, building signs, and other manifestations of an organization can either cost a great deal and take years or, if skilfully handled, be accomplished fairly quickly at no vast expense. Organization and planning become very important. In their work plan the designers should demonstrate that they are qualified to guide a company in this unusual area.

Before work starts, client and designer should agree the objective, the method for its accomplishment, the timing, and the fees.

Following agreement, the first stage of work must be an appraisal of the situation existing today and the potential communication goals. Exactly what this entails must depend on the size and type of organization. Design Research Unit took eighteen months to establish their first main recommendations for an organization as complex as British Rail. Henrion took the same time to arrive at recommendations for the Post Office, another immense (400,000 employees) and complex public service in the midst of a basic reorganization from government department to public corporation. As an indication of the design and identity problem: telephone kiosks are controlled by fifteen departments; they bear no relation to the organization for letterboxes, which appear in the same streets. It takes time to come to grips with complicated organizations, and one must understand them thoroughly to make good proposals. Rio Tinto-Zinc, for example, thought it would be necessary to allow designers two years to get to know the organization. The problem is not size, although RT-Z is one of the biggest mining organizations in the world, but political complexity. It has three layers of well-known companies. Learning how to clarify this, to convey correct impressions, takes time.

But these are exceptions. On the whole it is as much a mistake to overestimate the time required as to underestimate it. A sense of purpose and momentum ought to be established. To expect the initial orientation phase to take between four and eight months is appropriate in most cases.

During this 'orientation' phase, the role of the company executive responsible is to make available all the information the designers require. This entails providing research evidence, and arranging meetings. Though this may sound trivial it is not. For one thing, the designers will want to penetrate deep into the organization, and this invariably means meeting people situated in a number of plants about the country. Tying all these interviews together can be a real help. An executive with Allied International Designers, once interviewed twenty-seven people in eight locations in the Netherlands in one week. Working for a Swedish company, the same designers established an 'orientation team' of five people to conduct interviews with company executives all over Europe. The client executive can also help by suggesting people to meet for political reasons: in many organizations individuals have an influence that is unrelated to their position and it's worth knowing who these are. While the main board of a company may approve a design scheme, it will often live or die according to the way it is received lower down. It is imperative that the opinion should be sought of all those who will have to handle the design scheme. Not only is a sense of involvement important, but genuine participation is helpful.

So the designers handling this task should meet as many people as possible who can cast light on the situation of the company, and whose help will be wanted. It is good to ask them all general questions, but to be sure to distinguish between the expert and non-expert answer. For example, most people in a company have views about the advertising policy, but not all opinions have the same validity. This may be stating the obvious, but it is astonishing how often the obvious is not seen.

The designers must try to form a picture of how the organization stands now; to do this they need to understand the fields in which the company is operating, its competitors, its customers, and its problems. It is a mistake for a company to present its designers with only the glossy public statement, so easily seen through. As a consultant, the designer becomes an extension of the company: he needs to hear the truth and sincerely held opinions. Reliable designers will always treat such information confidentially. In this field it is to be remembered that one is dealing both with fact and fancy. What people believe is important, whether right or not.

While the views of people inside a company are of great interest, the problems of communicating with them are unlike the difficulties of reaching the majority outside. Their views must be weighted accordingly.

It is important to get opinions from people outside the company. Editors of trade journals, wholesalers, retailers, users of the company's products can all throw a light on the company. Few firms have conducted any image research; where they have it should certainly be studied. Assuming there is time, one should decide whether to conduct a formal image study to determine impartial attitudes to the company. This is said with some hesitation for four reasons: first, having arrived at this point, the company knows something is amiss; second, unless the researchers know what they're looking for, there's a danger that samples will need to be large and results sketchy; third, the experienced designer of corporate identities can, in fact, quickly pick up impressions and shades of feeling by looking and listening with care; fourth, essentially, the concern is with the future. While the present position of a company is, of course, relevant, one is looking forward to a changed situation where present research may be less helpful.

There are exceptions to this. At a brand level or in the case of a company with one kind of product, comparative studies *vis-à-vis* competitors can be fairly precise and rewarding. Informed respondents can be found with relative ease, they can comment on practical facts (the products, delivery times, etc.); they need not be asked hypothetical or theoretical questions they're ill equipped to answer.

Examples do exist, however, of careful and successful research projects that provide evidence of lasting value to the organizations which commission them. As knowledge of the need increases and techniques improve, basic image research will be more usual. Well done, it can be of great value, notably when dealing in other countries where, as we have seen, fundamental attitudes may be unlike anything one expects. As a random example, it is interesting to note the results of an image study conducted by the Swedish Chamber of Commerce in Belgium. Swedish products, it found, were considered of high quality, as one may have guessed. But Swedish design was not thought particularly good – a finding that runs counter to commonly-held opinion. For a Swedish company in Belgium to base its marketing on the calibre of its design, might not be the best course, this research suggests. This single example demonstrates the value that image research can have.

Research must be conducted by an independent agency, guided by the company's own research department and, in this case, by the designers who can say what they're looking for.

The 'orientation' stage falls into three parts. First, gathering facts and opinions from a variety of sources; second, analysing these facts and opinions; and third, drawing conclusions from them.

Even here you see the classic distinction between analytical and creative thought. Only by recognizing the difference can one maximize either. To describe the existing situation in wonderful detail without drawing conclusions for the future is to be wanting in perception. The most important contribution designers can make to an organization is to help point the directions it should move in: creative imagination can help to do this.

A simple, but model, example occurred when Lyons Bakery were changing their identity. Managed by John Ramsden and John Kerridge, the approach was classic. First, the company conducted an independent research programme to see what people thought of it, and what kind of products people would like to have from such a company. As might be expected, freshness, hygiene, moistness, and other qualities were named. These, in addition to the 'friendliness' we've already spoken of, became the brief for the designers. But they, looking through the research, became more and more convinced that one of the qualities sought by customers was 'bounty' – a generosity more normally thought of with home-cooking than factory-baking. This target was written into the brief. When the initial design work was done, yet more research was used to check whether the brief had been satisfied.

Since one is looking forward, it is vital to ask about the future. It is astounding how few companies have any serious long-term planning, or can point with confidence to their objectives year by year. Nonetheless, this is where the company's knowledge of its markets, and the chairman or managing director's own vision, is essential. It is for the designers to ask the questions and form the hypotheses. At this crucial stage, forecasting is desirable, coupled with perception and imagination.

In the fact-finding stage, it is wise for designers to meet the most senior officers last – not only because less time will be wasted but also because from the earlier meetings theories will have emerged, and these can be discussed with senior executives before being hardened into written recommendations.

Before any design work starts, the information gathered will be written up. This should be quite a short report to the company, restating the objective, and noting some of the factors relating to it. It should then state the recommended *communication goals*. The statement should be concise. It should say exactly how the company wishes to be understood; it is the kernel of all the work done so far, the essence of everything that will follow. For this reason it is worth poring over, worth getting exactly right.

The statement should be submitted to the main board, together with a written report which should outline any difficult questions to be resolved and suggest ways of tackling them.

Sometimes the report is presented with visual design recommendations. There may be special reasons for this (once more illustrating the need to treat each case on its merits). As a general rule, though, it is best to have the written report presented first, to make sure the client agrees with the thought process proposed before the design work starts. There are several reasons for suggesting this. One is to see that the correct problems have been defined and are being solved, if for no other reason than to avoid having designers busily solving the wrong ones. Another is to satisfy both client and designer that the designers have the right brief (for this document, once approved, becomes the formal working brief). Yet another, not to be underrated, is to try to cut down the amount of personal taste involved. In a written statement there is little avenue for the expression or imposition of taste, but it covers almost all the important design decisions that will be taken.

Should a company be seen as traditional or modern? Small or large? International or local? Should it have a symbol or not? Should the company retain existing logotypes or not? Should the design convey graceful femininity or solidity? All these decisions and more can be arrived at by careful analysis and good projection. While it is wrong to tell a designer *how* to accomplish

Corporate identity need not be so serious, nor need companies only strive to look large. When Smiths Food Group decided to open a number of quick chicken restaurants, they made the name more informal – Smithy's Kitchen – and they introduced a gay chef to all manifestations of the operation.

The Bakery Division of J Lyons and Company was found by research to be thought too large, impersonal, and unfriendly. As steps to make the company smaller, the name was changed to Lyons Bakery – at once simpler and less formal – and the now familiar 'bowl and whisk' symbol was introduced to link the company with an idea of baking familiar to every housewife.

the sought-after results, the purpose of the brief should be to tell him *what* to accomplish. This helps client as much as designers.

It is sometimes thought that information inhibits creativity. Clients are reluctant to tell too much in case they restrict the designer. This laudable motive arises from a misunderstanding of the creative process: you can't expect a designer to solve a problem unless he knows what the problem is. (So much for the speculative presentations advertising agencies are asked to make to new clients.) Equally, it is hard for a client to judge the solution to a problem unless he, too, knows what problem is being solved.

The report, written before designing starts, thus performs the invaluable task of putting client and designer on the same wavelength. When creative work is presented, they will both have written criteria to judge it by, they will see much more nearly through the same eyes than their different experiences would lead one to expect.

The 'design platform' should be discussed by client and designer and agreed in detail. This is the time to argue and modify. Often such design platforms specify more clearly than has been possible before what the next steps should be – not only overall communication goals but also some specific areas to work on.

The client should approve the proposals formally when he is completely satisfied. They then become the brief to which the designers will work.

What has happened so far? From a general wish to review their corporate communications, a company has appointed designers, agreed a programme of work, and arrived at a detailed professional analysis of the problem, together with specific written recommendations for future action.

While we're dealing here with visual communications, there is no reason why these recommendations need be too restricted. For example, a specific recommendation given by designers to one of Europe's main cement manufacturers was the institution of a programme of employee relations. A food company was advised to shorten its product range. A paper firm was advised to diversify its range to enter what were predicted to be future growth markets. The same company was advised to shift from being known as a primary producer to being known as a manufacturer of converted products. Five years ago a British brewery was advised by its designers to widen the role of the public house and shift people's understanding of it. They rejected the advice and now, with stricter driving laws reinforcing predictable changes in social behaviour, regret it.

The designer's appraisal should be penetrating and far-sighted. Trying to determine how a company should position itself must involve thoughts of the future. Evidence suggests that this forward look by independent, imaginative people can be of substantial interest and value to a company busy with day-to-day worries. Only when a design platform is agreed can creative design work begin.

This may seem to be exceeding the designer's brief: his job is to design. The deeper view, however, is that if a company wants to seem right it must *be* right, and that designers, if they are competent to comment on corporate communications, must be free at least to question corporate policy. Three reasons are clear. First, image and reality must be integrated. Second, independent designers, properly trained and experienced, concerned with the future, have a wide, overall view of inevitable developments in business and are occasionally even more keenly aware of competitive threats than the clients they serve. Third, we are moving into an age when corporate policy will be influenced by the impact it has on public and industrial relations. Companies will do things and stop doing things because they have repercussions among workers, staff, the trade, or consumers. For the adviser on an important aspect of corporate communications to be barred from such considerations, is to neglect an area that will become more central as time goes by.

It is easy to illustrate how design runs all through modern industry. The five areas of corporate policy-making (marketing, product development, personnel, communications, and finance) each involve design judgement. In the marketing area, the design of products, packaging, display material, printed matter, advertising, and even architecture affects not only immediate sales, but longer-term attitudes to the company. Product development obviously includes design and also has long-term communication implications, and so on. Even financial decisions may be influenced by communication requirements. Should the PR department be expanded? Should the new office building be acquired solely on the basis of its rent, without consideration of the effect it has on employees, visitors, or passing public? This is not to support wasteful 'prestige' premises, solely to suggest that there are more than financial considerations, and to that extent financial decisions are affected.

It is to suggest, too, that to be most effective corporate identity consultants should probe deeply and be ready to make apparently irrelevant comments, if they see the relevance to the task for which they are appointed.

5

How the Woolmark was designed – and other symbols

Even with a clear brief, the designer's job has just begun. Weeks of experiment, of effort, and disappointment go into creating anything as simple as good corporate identity requires. Simplicity is essential for a company symbol that must have immediate impact and yet lasting effect. It can't be fussy if it's to work on the side of a lorry and on a twenty-five-year pin; it can't be ultra-fashionable if it's to last decades. Achieving this simplicity takes time.

People are sometimes disappointed to see a simple squiggle after waiting several months. That it is the right squiggle is proven only over a period of time. Creating good symbols is like the leader-writer on a newspaper who said, 'It will have to be a long editorial tonight. I haven't time to write a short one.' The Woolmark is an example. Launched in 1964, it is internationally famous. Used on 10 million labels a month, licensed (at the end of 1967) by 9500 manufacturers throughout the world, and the subject of an estimated £65 million promotion campaign over 5 years, the Woolmark has the necessary virtue of extreme simplicity. It consists of 15 lines, curved on 3 arcs – as simple as that. But the symbol, by Italian designer Francesco Saroglia, took time to perfect. He started with paper strips printed with a cross-hatching of black and white. He twisted them various ways. Always, he says, the cross-hatching broke the flow line. He tried stripes – first a simple knot; he found it too stiff – 'not suggestive of a softly draping, subtle fabric'. He tried again with a bow pattern; this time the lines swung gracefully, but the ends and folds made a severe outline. Again and again he tried. Then he noticed how a mirror bent the lines, 'like a fisherman's spear bending at the water's surface'. From this idea he developed a three-dimensional model in which an endless quintet of stripes wound into a pyramidal solid. With this on his desk Saroglia produced the Woolmark, flattening the convolutions into a simple design that retained the intriguing quality of his model. It looks well both in neon 50 feet across, and in fine stitching on a worsted fabric.

When Michael Russell, who created the admired Lyons Bakery bowl and whisk, presented a design for a new mark to the Spillers food group, they wanted to see how he had arrived at his easy answer. He showed them 250 sheets of rough designs.

Karen Munck, who created the new identity for the Smiths Food Group, arrived at her solution by patient analysis of the existing identity. She tried and eliminated the diamond shape they'd used for fifty years; she found that not only was it wasteful of space and too static but also, being a generic shape, lacking in uniqueness. Then she focused her attention on the red and blue stripes used on the old packages. These were much more easily recognized than the diamond. She worked on them for several weeks, creating many degrees of abstraction before arriving at the almost rudimentary arrangement now used – three horizontal red and three vertical blue stripes over the name 'Smiths'.

The late Jim Nash, in New York, went through the same cycle when he redesigned the H J Heinz identity some years ago. The trademark at that time was a pickle. The 'Pennsylvania Keystone' shape, bordered by green and gold, was the main feature on can labels. Inside the keystone shape, which occupied all the front face, were the name 'Heinz', the name, description, and weight of contents, the slogan '57 Varieties', and the name and address of the company. Trying many variations, now preserved on some 200 slides, he eventually finished with the keystone with 'Heinz' and '57' contained in it. These three important recognition devices, concentrated together, became the new identity for the company.

These examples are quoted to show that it is harder than it looks. You don't *have* to fill many sketch-pads before a good design emerges, but it is likely. It is not part of this book to describe the creative process,[1] and anyway, people work in many different ways. Designers must be given time: their efforts must be directed to solving specific problems, and this means that they should not fall into the common trap of working up one pet solution too soon. There is a lot to be said for developing a number of rough ideas first before becoming emotionally involved in any one of them. The rigours of designing a successful corporate identity are such that eliminating designs at an early stage is not difficult. Taste enters into such judgements, but there are many practical points to meet which tend to become the main considerations.

In any design organization, it is normal for preliminary sketches to be seen by a review board in the company. The same board reviews work again at a later stage. These formal reviews are in addition to the daily cross-currents of discussion that go into any project. The review board performs the useful function of letting experienced and objective people see and criticize the development in time to influence it. This kind of design must attract the uninformed no less than the initiated, it is valuable, therefore, to let people see it who are not directly involved in its creation. One design company exposes its proposed designs to a panel of independent 'informed opinion'. This may include an advertising agent, someone from the Council of Industrial Design, an architect, a PRO, a representative of a consumer association, and others.

At a basic level, a visual identity may consist of a symbol or logotype, a letterstyle, and a colour scheme. Each must be chosen with extreme care. In more complex cases, the problems to be solved call for the widest experience and best judgement available. Supporting the designer in a design organization will be people expert in marketing, advertising, organization, finance, and in any large corporate identity programme all their skills are utilized. When Allied International Designers work on the communication problems of a large manufacturer their team may include all these skills, sometimes starting with marketing and research consultants, perhaps using their architects to advise on buildings, someone to advise on the internal design organization in the client company, perhaps someone advising on advertising applications, a print consultant, specialists in working drawings, a photography studio, and others. To reconcile all their diverse experience into a simple scheme, clearly calls for many meetings and tight planning. Here is more evidence of the iceberg nature of corporate communication work.

What makes a good corporate identity? When a scheme is laid before you, how do you judge it? What should company and designer be aiming at?

A good corporate identity is one that will identify and express the personality of the corporation as it will be when the scheme is substantially in use. This should be appropriate to the market and audiences defined by the company. Once more it should be emphasized that good design is no substitute for good performance. Poor products stay on the shelves no matter how many design awards the manufacturer may have won.

The mental attitude that allows a good design policy to be created in the first place, and the discipline necessary to follow it through, themselves help to stimulate good performance. There is a quality of leadership about corporate communications. It can provide standards for people to strive for. People mostly live up to standards set for them if the standards are capable of accomplishment. In this sense, a good corporate identity can help improve actual performance. But great care should be taken to distinguish between legitimate reaching forward and dishonest overstatement.

Notice that the definition of a 'good corporate identity' speaks not only of identifying the corporation, but also of expressing its personality. This is a paramount distinction. Also, it makes the point that the personality to express is the one that will exist at some future time. Changing markets, changing product ranges, changing organizations, increasingly concentrated

Symbols have to work many ways. This must be an important consideration at the earliest design stage. A random selection of uses, shown here, includes (a) the identification of a tractor; (b) a symbol shaped in plastic; (c) cut in stone; (d) used as paper decorations (for the Canadian Arthritic Society); (e) on a helicopter for David Brown, the engineering group; and (f) sewn on a uniform.

competition, coupled with the length of time it takes to implement a thorough scheme, force the abandonment of instant, short-term attitudes.

We have seen how necessary it is to understand the broad relationship between the corporation and its publics (whether the 'corporation' is a government department, local council, or a business), and how one must try to determine which qualities are required of the organization. That such research is helpful is clear enough. While it is neither possible nor desirable to be all things to all men, we've noted how different groups of people require different virtues from an organization. The employee wants one thing, customers another, shareholders something else. That is one dimension of variation necessary in a good corporate identity.

F H K Henrion and Alan Parkin describe another. They argue:

> There is a spectrum of tones of voice appropriate to different kinds of items. At the loud end of the spectrum are advertising, signs, vehicles and retail packaging. These are normally seen in brief glimpses amongst highly competitive surroundings and have to shout to attract attention. In the middle of the spectrum are most of the stationery and publications which though temporary in use, can take for granted the main attention of the person, and need only moderate emphasis to do their job of reinforcing the image. At the quiet end are the items in long-term use – durable products, buildings (as distinct from signs and displays they may carry) and furnishings. Here any over-emphasis becomes increasingly irritating as time goes by.[2]

One might challenge parts of this statement, but it does show one more degree of flexibility.

These two examples of the need to say different things, and to say them in different ways, underline the flexibility a good corporate identity must possess. The fastest way to be recognized is to show exactly the same face repetitively, without variation. For a politician to be seen now with glasses, now without, now with a hat, now bareheaded, is to reduce recognition, as Britain's pipe-smoking, Gannex-coated Premier realized. Many highly effective corporate identities maintain extreme consistency. London Transport, for instance, use consistently a two-colour symbol, a standard and very clear letterstyle. Slight variations are permitted in printed matter and posters, but these are always identified correctly. Shell, the most international oil company in the world, went to the extent of placing its pecten on a standard red background, to counter the variations of setting for the symbol provided by its environment. Think of KLM, Christian Dior, VW, Coca Cola, Esso: all excellent, all constant.

It can be argued that these lack flexibility and that where a company is dominant in its market, there is a risk of monotony. In fact, the IBM identity, widely quoted and much respected, is based on a high degree of flexibility. When Tom Watson, then president and now chairman, retained Eliot Noyes as his design consultant he asked: 'Why not create a corporate design theme

Good design, to be effective, should run through industry, helping to establish a co-ordinated corporate personality. This chart shows the main areas of board responsibility (plus finance) and suggests that design relates to them all. It is interesting to note the position of architecture (here called environment) as a function of communication, marketing, and personnel relations.

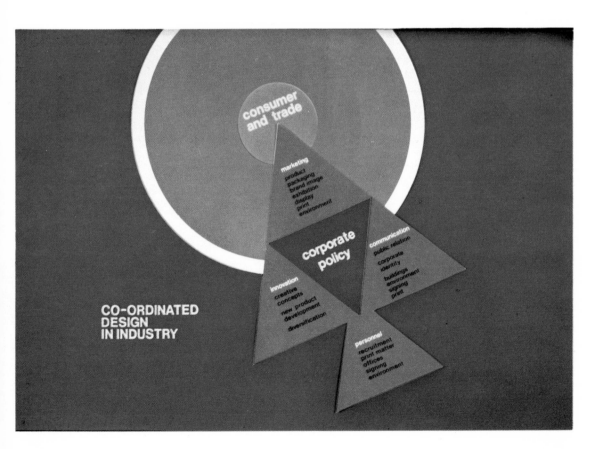

What people thought of these symbols

	D&B (shield)	DB (new)
Food	**16%**	—
Clothes	**10%**	—
Engineering	**2%**	**28%**

(a) Research was conducted into the old symbol used by David Brown (a high-quality engineering group) and three new symbols designed for the group. It showed only 2 per cent of people interviewed correctly identified the business of the company, despite the symbol's use for years. Twenty-eight per cent of the people interviewed correctly identified the business represented by the new symbol although they had never seen it before. No other figures were significant.

(b) People interviewed were then asked to put the four symbols tested into a rating scale. Results showed the old symbol was seen as representing a poor-quality, backward but friendly company. The new symbol was seen to represent the highest quality, most progressive, most advanced, and scientifically based company, but which was not particularly friendly. It reveals the efficacy of non-verbal communications, but also underlines attitudes to old and new companies which must be taken into account.

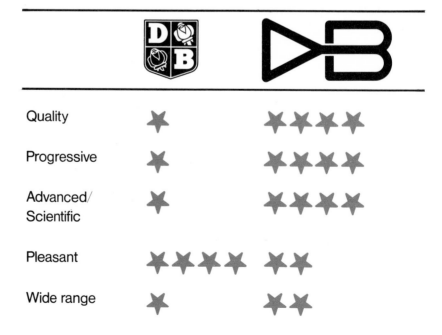

Swissair and Air Canada (the name was changed from Trans-Canada Airways as it became more international) both use national symbols, even though Swissair is privately owned. Air Canada design by Stewart & Morrison. Corporate communications should be reviewed regularly. After using a well-applied scheme for eight years BEA changed. The red and white arrow on a blue background, obviously taken from the Union Jack, expresses a national airline dynamically. It is neither stiff, static, nor solemn as national emblems may be.

Redesigned recently, the new Mobil corporate identity reduces the Flying Red Horse (useful when radio was the most effective advertising medium) to a passing link and concentrates on a striking expression of the short, unique, appropriate name.

– a distinctive colour, a common motif?' In that way, it was thought, everything 'from a matchbook to a monumental building' would become part of an integrated whole. Noyes, it is said, vigorously opposed the idea. He contended that any theme, any device is doomed to become hackneyed and dated. IBM's design programme, he urged, should have only two constants: it should reflect quality, and it should be contemporary.

In this ambition IBM has been brilliantly successful, but it is fair to say that few firms would have been able to do the same. The essential consistency has come in other ways. The chairman has consistently believed in good design and supported it. Eliot Noyes has, for twelve years now, consistently acted as 'consultant director of design' (even the title is indicative). They have between them consistently employed the best designers and architects. In architecture, for example, the late Eero Saarinen, designer of the US Embassies in London and Oslo, designed several buildings for them. Charles Eames has designed films and exhibits for IBM. Paul Rand designed the graphics of the new identity.

IBM standards exist for all to follow. Each graphics designer is issued with a manual that shows elements of the house style. The corporate logotype has been standardized, as have nameplates for machines. A standard style of type is a connecting thread in all printed matter. Created in seven different locations, it is hard to coordinate product design, but some rules have been established, and there are quarterly coordinating meetings.

The company believes:

. . . standards are no substitute for creativity . . . and the only real standard imposed is the standard of high quality.

This philosophy is attractive. Who would deny an enthusiasm for quality? It has been followed successfully by others. The Pirelli building in Milan has the same spirit of original excellence as the company's calenders or transport posters. Olivetti had this excellence running from product to package, factory to store fitting. Braun, in Germany, in the years before it was acquired by Gillette, earned an international reputation by design out of all proportion to the volume of its sales. Writing of this, Richard Moss in the US magazine *Industrial Design*, said:

Every Braun design seems to obey three basic laws: the law of order, the law of harmony, and the law of economy.

A Braun corporate image emerged not by imposing an outside discipline, but by the development of a philosophy.

Examine these cases, or the handful of others that could be quoted, and you will see a tremendous dependence on the calibre of client and designer, and on the continuity of their trusting association.

Aspirants to this philosophy should be warned of the practical hazards. Who is to set the standards of excellence? If there is an argument between sales director and designer, who wins? If excellence costs more, is that a cost the company is willing to bear, and report to shareholders? It has been said that most taxpayers are as capable of grand passion as they are of grand opera. Maybe they are as capable of great design. While the modern corporation should strive for high standards, it should do so within a realistic understanding of its own framework.

This estimate of what is practical in the organization should certainly influence the designer. One reason for failure is trying to push the company further than it is willing to go. Designer Raymond Loewy speaks of a MAYA stage for design – 'Most Advanced Yet Acceptable'. And probably all designers have had the dual experience of companies that want to improve as long as it doesn't mean altering anything, and of genuinely ambitious executives who find themselves unable to push through the changes they want. Aesthetic judgements should be left to designers, but they seldom are. Even so, a criterion of corporate identity is certainly its practicality.

A cardinal requirement of a corporate identity is that it will work wherever it is applied. This is a rudimentary requirement, yet it is surprising how often it is underrated or misunderstood. For example, the old David Brown symbol, a quartered shield with the white rose of Yorkshire and red rose of Lancashire, really only worked in four colours. In press advertising the shield became an inky smudge. Yet still some preferred it.

This inevitable need to function in black and white casts doubt on symbols designed in several colours. They may look fine under ideal conditions, but when conditions are less than ideal they stop working. Client companies should always satisfy themselves that the designs put to them show the proposed identity in black and white, and in various sizes. Fine filigree design may be splendid on a presentation board. But will it work on a cap badge or twenty-five-year pin? Will it be seen adequately under adverse conditions, in poor light, or at high speed?

Will the proposed design be easy to stamp, etch, carve, or mould on metal (product nameplates, badges, door signs)? Can it be sewn or printed on cloth (flags, overalls, uniforms, ties, labels)? Can it be built into huge electric signs, stencilled on crates, transferred onto vehicles? Printed on poor surfaces (shipping cases, gummed tape, premium offers)? Will the design pass local authorities and town planners (some colours are difficult)?

All these are practical requirements which skilled corporate identity designers know about and design for. They stress the need for design which is simple and robust in structure, though this need not mean lacking in refinement. In this design work one must look ahead to potential future uses of the identity. The Albert Heijn symbol, for example, was designed to work on television, even though commercial TV did not exist in the Netherlands at that time.

Another practical requirement of a corporate identity is that it should be capable of being applied consistently with or without the original designers' help. This means defining standards for use (which we will consider later). It also means that relationships should be established between symbol and letterstyle, to suit likely commercial requirements as well as space available.

It is here that the designer can provide opportunity for what might be called 'controlled flexibility'.

The experience of Charrington United Breweries is relevant. This brewery, now merged with another and owning 11,000 public houses in Britain, felt the need both for a consistent look and for variety. Variety was needed for two reasons: first, the architecture of their pubs varies vastly. It was necessary to provide the group's own local architects with a choice of design and colour schemes for signing which would suit any building. Architecture owned by the group ranged from thatched cottage to housing-estate brick. It included Victorian Dutch gable, mock Parthenon, pseudo-Gothic, and all the rest. Second, such is England, that there are often several Charrington pubs in the same short road. Alternative design schemes were thought necessary to avoid monotony. Their consultant designers created standards for these variations.

It is inherent in the nature of symbolism that the relationships between name and symbol may want to alter as time passes. It takes time for new symbols to become known. Early on, they need to be supported by the name to which they refer. This relationship may be reversed as the symbol becomes known. Here we find a reference again to time – a factor never to be forgotten in corporate communications work. Whatever is created must be flexible enough to suit various conditions now, and possibly different ones in the future.

The overriding need for an identity to last affects design substantially. In the main, the designer of corporate identities must eschew current fashion. He must see through and beyond it.

An understanding of time cycles is important to effective design. That people buy cornflakes once or twice a week, and computers once every three, five, or ten years, influences the design requirements of each. This, by the way, can help explain the various degrees of excitement you see in good identities: what is bright and exciting today may become a bore tomorrow. Few things separate the skilled designer of corporate identities from the amateur more than this appreciation of time. Mostly, the good designer's work has to last for years and be seen thousands of times; this certainly influences its basic character.

Self-evident requirements of any identity are that it should be appropriate, recognizable, memorable, and unique. The scale of relative importance depends on the particular situation and, to some extent, on the way the identity is used. It is hard to overstate the importance of the context in which a design is seen, or the consistency of its use. They must relate to the qualities mentioned. Nonetheless, they remain qualities to seek. Any man judging a proposed corporate identity should ask whether these virtues exist when the design is seen in context.

It is fashionable now for designers to refer to the *Gestalt* which, taken from the German language of psychology, refers to the whole design in context. The *Concise Oxford Dictionary* defines *Gestalt* as: 'an organized whole in which each individual part affects every other, the whole being more than a sum of its parts'.

While we have referred mostly to the use of symbolism to convey ideas one must not for a moment think of it as existing in isolation. The speed of modern communication is such that we may expect a continuing effort to be made to concentrate identity into as few elements as possible. And certainly both laboratory research and market research have established the efficacy of symbolism. In our TV-dominated, visual world, there is no sign this will decrease. Even so, it is the total environment in which a company is seen that will distinguish and characterize it.

The advantage of a symbol is that it can be unique. It can be registered. Colours, highly effective as they are, on the whole cannot be claimed as the property of any one company and therefore cannot be considered unique. In West Germany it is legally possible for a company to claim the use of a certain colour in its field, but hardly anywhere else in the world is this so. The immediate implication is that an organization is unwise to rely too much on colour for recognition. Many companies misunderstand this and cloak poor symbols in strong colour schemes. In this sense, they are secure only as long as competitors choose to let them remain so. This is not to say that colour should be ignored. On the contrary, it can be a most valuable aid to communication, and should certainly be chosen for its appropriateness. For example, the 1000 vehicles of Lyons Bakery are white, with a contrasting warm, tan colour. The white was deliberately chosen to help convey the cleanliness of this food firm. Colour influences the *Gestalt*. So, while every effort should be made to use colour consistently to help convey impressions, one should take care it does not become the overriding identifying feature.

The choice of a typeface can also help identify and convey impressions. But the main job of print is to be read. Legibility is much more important than any strained originality.

Nonetheless, the choice of typeface can contribute to the total impression of an organization. Light or bold, flowing or static, it adds something to the picture. One of the most interesting 'corporate identity' projects recently has been the work of Peter Hatch for the 108-year-old Royal Opera House in Covent Garden. Using Baskerville, a full, flowing typeface, he has created a visual character for the opera and its associated companies based entirely on typography. But this is rare.

Thus, we see the role of the symbol or logotype as the main identifying device, supported by an appropriate use of colour and typography – the whole creating the *Gestalt* people recognize.

It would be wrong to infer that symbols are imperative. Sometimes they just get in the way. A good example occurred in 1967, when Marabou, the Swedish chocolate firm, decided to coordinate and improve its visual communications. They had recognized that, although they are the biggest and best-known company in their field in Scandinavia, they needed to increase their business abroad where they were less known; they also expected more competition at home from foreign companies also widening their markets. 'Marabou' is the name of a scavenging bird, a West African stork. Appropriate or not, that's the name. To reinforce it, the company had used an illustration of the bird on every wrapper, every slab of chocolate, every vehicle. Although it was poorly used, the bird was always there, and undoubtedly recognition was divided to some extent between the bird and the name. Karen Munck who tackled the problem, felt the bird was a hindrance. She dropped it. Instead, she concentrated all attention on the name. Marabou has a good sound and it works internationally. In advertising, on cinema screens, and in supporting press, the company had a famous actress saying, 'M.m.m. . . . Marabou,' as she munched a bar of chocolate. This had become well known. The designer created a letterstyle for the full name which was full, flowing, and fluid in character. The initial 'M' she used for the 'M.m.m.m. . . .' In her presentation, she showed how in some circumstances the initial 'M' alone could work. Here the whole identity has been concentrated, to great effect, on the name. In time, the name of this extremely modern and well-run company will become totally divorced from any connection with the scavenging bird, in the same way as Shell has ceased to mean a shell found on a beach.

Marabou is a company where the deliberate communications had accidentally fallen behind performance. With good-quality products, very good employee relations policies, good offices (among the best examples of *bureaulandschaft* planning in Europe) and an enviable reputation for enlightened art patronage, they are a model of the modern corporation – good all round. Their new visual identity will help pull these strands together in public awareness.

Chase Manhattan Bank decided to build a very modern, high, and elegant building for themselves in the solidly traditional Wall Street area of New York. They wanted to make their progressiveness clear. At the same time they picked two young designers, Ivan Chermayeff and Emil Antonucci, to carry this through to all the other expressions of the bank. The starting-point was a symbol. They were using a hybrid made from two old symbols used by previous companies (Chase National and the Bank of the Manhattan Company merged in 1955). Their joint symbol included a globe, a map of the United States, a name, a slogan.

Criteria the bank chose for a new visual identity were: uniqueness, simplicity, and 'usability'. They ruled out using bits of the old symbol and agreed to make a fresh start. They decided against monograms since, according to the bank executive most heavily involved:

> In a period of mergers and other changes in the banking scene it was always possible the name of the institution might be altered.

This is a most important comment. They wanted the new symbol to suggest stability and progress. They saw that it should work in black and white and in colour; that it should be recognizable in the smallest print sizes, yet interesting enough when used large on buildings.

The symbol they chose was abstract. As one might expect they had trouble, chiefly internally, getting it accepted. One way they overcame this was to print a card showing the symbol and explaining it. They pointed out that the symbol is:

> a simple yet powerful geometric form embodying a strong feeling of motion and activity . . . it is divided in such a way as to suggest forward motion within the framework of control. . . . It has a modern appearance, at the same time its octagonal shape is reminiscent of ancient coins. . . .

Now Chase Manhattan Bank use their symbol on all advertising, buildings, stationery, and a host of promotion items (cufflinks, earrings, playing cards, key chains, cigarette lighters, ties, packets of golf tees, trays, paperweights). They have established a clear design manual and, with Peter Gee, a British-born designer, modular principles for all printed matter. The purpose of this modular system, the bank executive explains, is to:

> enable us to maintain an overall design discipline while permitting a certain amount of flexibility.

The modular system is not intended to be an instant design formula, but they find it useful for work that has to be legible, effective, and quickly produced. Such a modular system can be a valuable tool in bringing unity to a house style.

Does it all work? Each year, Chase Manhattan conducts an independent survey on symbol recognition. In five years, the percentage of respondents identifying the new symbol correctly has grown from 13 to 48 per cent.

It is important to say that this activity has not been isolated, but is part of a total communications programme. The cartoon in the *New Yorker* (page 162) is a small indication of what can be accomplished.

If one were to list the do's and don'ts of corporate communications, these two aims would appear high among the 'do's': first, to create a policy that is true to the company and the situation in which it will find itself. Second, that anything done should flow through all channels of the company and all methods of communication – varying to suit conditions and audiences, but essentially constant. These are different from, but support, the theory of *Gestalt*. All manifestations of a company should be seen as contributions to its personality and to the impressions it conveys. Image formation is a complex process in which numerous manifestations, each in itself of seemingly small value, contribute to the final result. This is a point made by Shell in a book they published on this subject. They also said:

> These countless elements, often inter-related, project the company's personality, the individuality of its brand. But all this is modified by competitor's activity and by extraneous influences . . . so that what is ultimately registered in the public mind is often a distortion of the intended projection. The company is not necessarily seen as it sees itself.

The cautionary note is an argument not for pessimism, but rather for a realistic appraisal of the scale of the problem. Only by purposeful and consistent communication can the modern organization, struggling in a complex and competitive environment, hope to put itself across accurately and well.

REFERENCES

1. James Pilditch. 'How to be more creative', in *The Silent Salesman*, Business Pbns., 1959.
2. *Design Coordination and Corporate Image*, Studio Vista, 1967.

Can market research
check design?

It is a curious, even dangerous, phenomenon of our times that an ounce of research is considered of more worth than a pound of qualified opinion. The danger lies in the single word 'research', embracing the most sophisticated techniques of national samples, of continuous retail and consumer audits, of motivational, optical, and attitudinal research, all of which can have great value, and amateur questionnaires, which are useless. This is a subject to be treated with caution. It is here because research results can influence the course of design activity.

Designers and clients should welcome good research at all stages of a corporate identity project: at the beginning, to define the need; when design is created, to confirm its effectiveness; and later, to check its results. But they should insist on good research, conducted by qualified agencies, and they should heed the cautious statements of these research specialists.

This needs to be said because there are still many manufacturers and designers who abuse the trust placed in research. In 1968 one still heard cases of clients inviting employees into a room to choose which of several designs they preferred. One still heard of designers passing off amateur tricks as research to prove the value of their work.

The temptation arises not only because the subtleties of good research are not recognized or respected, but also because qualified judgement is undervalued.

Compagnie d'Esthétique Industrielle in Paris, when they are brought in to study a problem, find out what information the client has on the problem.

'What is your current image as far as you know?' they ask. They may suggest using research but their creative director is cautious about this.

> It is hard to get research you can use in design terms, or to get information that projects into the future, . . .

which he believes it must do. The design company's own staff brief any research companies, and they also analyse the results. Their conclusions, they find, may differ from those of the researchers. What they try to do is to arrive at a simple statement of a general theme that everyone can agree, in this way everyone is after the same goal.

CEI's concern about the future, incidentally, expresses itself even earlier. They like to write their own brief.

> If you leave the brief to the client, he often forgets the future, or tends to be too restrictive. We know the kind of information we need to do a job.

Allied International Designers believe strongly in the need for as much prior information as possible. A standard question, at the start of any corporate identity programme would always be to ask what research information is available. On several occasions it has been necessary to have some research done into the position of the company, in communication terms, vis-à-vis its audiences and competitors. The belief is that it is important to know where the company stands today, to define its real communication problems, to pinpoint real needs (capable of being accomplished) before the most effective design work can start.

Designers who once resisted this invasion of their creative or intuitive domain, now not only welcome research information but feel it a necessary prerequisite. 'How can you tell the time,' they ask, 'without a watch?' To design in a vacuum is always a little frightening.

A Canadian paper firm, interested in entering the British market, once employed a package design unit to undertake a study for them. 'But,' protested the designers, 'we are not researchers.' The client replied, 'We can buy all the statistics we want. What we need are good opinions.'

Opinions of experienced designers have value. This is particularly true in two areas: first, their own metier and second, the future. It is extremely difficult to derive good postulations about the future by research alone. Since corporate communications are at least as concerned with the future as the present, and more than the past, this is something to remember.

It is no wish of the author to detract from the value of good research in any way. On the contrary, it is possible to hope and predict that research will be an essential part of corporate communication planning in the future. This chapter ends by quoting case histories where it has been of demonstrable benefit.

One must express a faith in the insight and instinctive foresight of good creative people. In the design world one sees (often enough to cease being surprised) genuine examples of future trends anticipated. In the scientific and rational world we live in, this human capacity tends to be devalued. Wise manufacturers will take care not to make this mistake. Curiously, there are cases where potentially good long-term corporate identities have future years taken off their lives by companies anxious to satisfy contemporary taste. Sometimes this is right, but sometimes, especially when it takes several years to put a new identity into circulation, it is quite wrong. The good designer by training, experience, and inclination can judge this.

Let's take a case where research has been of benefit to a corporate identity decision. The David Brown Corporation research has already been referred to. The problem was complicated. When the designers developed their solution, they created a number of new symbols which, they felt, might all work in varying ways. At the same time, they felt the need to measure the adequacy of the existing symbol. Some executives in the group were not dissatisfied with what they had. Indeed, the situation was not devoid of vested interests anxious to preserve the *status quo*.

The designers, on the instruction of the group PRO, appointed an independent research agency to test the existing symbol together with three new ones they had developed. The sample was small, but properly selected. It consisted of 165 AB males split into under/over 35, North/South England.

As a sample, this group was thought the most likely within the scale of the test to be potential customers of David Brown. But because, apart from Aston Martin cars, the group's products tend to be either industrially purchased or bought by farmers, both of which would know the group better, even this properly conducted test had to be viewed with caution. A bigger budget would have permitted more selective sampling. Even so, the results were useful. They showed, remarkably, that the existing symbol was identified with David Brown by only 2 per cent of the sample. When asked to say what kind of company respondents thought the existing symbol stood for, 16 per cent said a clothing company, 10 per cent said a food firm, and only 2 per cent said engineering. On the other hand, one of the new symbols, never before seen, was identified by 28 per cent of respondents as being the symbol of an engineering firm.

People were asked to put the symbols in order. They were asked which symbol they thought represented the most advanced company, the second most advanced company, and so on. Results showed that one of the new symbols was seen as representing the most advanced, the most scientifically based company with the highest-quality products. The existing symbol was thought to represent the least advanced, least scientifically based company with the worst products. But, interestingly, the roles were reversed when it came to being pleasant to deal with. People thought the company with the old symbol, the poor products, would be the nicest to deal with. Equally they thought the modern scientific company would not be pleasant to deal with.

This profile, reflecting almost classically the attitude towards little old firms against big new ones, provided the David Brown Corporation with a clear choice. The results of this research were presented together with the proposed design scheme, and undoubtedly helped the company judge whether to change over to the new identity. The research also pinpointed where to concentrate communication effort in the future.

That's an example of research being used to help a design presentation, adding great weight to it, making the decision easier. It is a policy to recommend even though, as any researcher says, there are limits to what one can hope to learn in this way about abstract symbols.

It is also possible to find out whether there are any drawbacks in a proposed symbol, and this is sometimes done. An example occurred when the executive of one company said the symbol proposed to him reminded him of a snake, and he always loathed snakes. On the face of it, this was a highly personal, irrational point of view. But many people share the same fear. If it could be found that the symbol reminded others of snakes, then that would be cause to drop it. A proper research exercise was conducted. Well over half the people interviewed (about 600 housewives) identified the type of company correctly, to the extent of judging its size and type of products it made, even though the symbol was abstract. None mentioned snakes.

When Lyons Bakery checked their symbol, it was mainly to see whether there were any negative associations. There were not. Indeed, over 70 per cent of the housewives interviewed identified the symbol as coming from a bakery: 'Friendly, with good fresh products, lots of butter, and cream.' Twelve per cent said it was a creamery.

These few results demonstrate the remarkable accuracy that is possible in completely non-verbal communication. Symbols alone tell the story. The research conducted is a modest enough cost if it provides the companies concerned with the assurance that they are doing right.

So far, we have seen two uses of research in corporate communication work: first, to help define problems; second, to check that the creative solutions work.

A third use of research is that a few companies need an identity that will work globally. They need to be assured before a final decision is taken that the proposed symbol can be registered globally and that it doesn't offend any religious, political, or other ideas anywhere. This kind of research takes time but is not difficult.

There is also a fourth use: to provide a feedback of information. We're concerned with communication, with conveying ideas and information from the organization to audiences within and beyond it. Continuing research can help us know how we're succeeding.

Asking people to judge symbols, must involve them in judgements beyond their normal experience. Sometimes it is practical to test new products or packages and from these, to deduce attitudes towards the company. An advantage of this is that one gets nearer the kind of judgement housewives are used to making.

Indeed, it is remarkable with what firmness one can draw image conclusions from such package research. An example occurred when the Smiths Food

Identification with your audiences. The public is a good deal more interested in education than in the proud accomplishments of almost any firm. This Ford advertisement is likely to be better appreciated than many so-called 'prestige' ads. It also teaches people about Ford and hopefully engenders good feeling towards the company.

STUDY

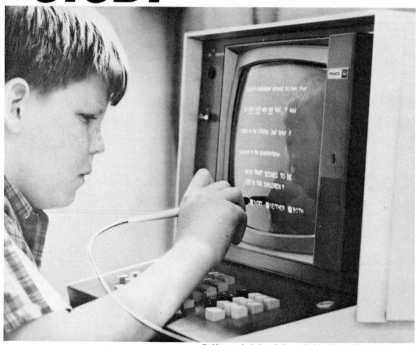

...has a better idea /**for education**

Problem: today's knowledge explosion gives teachers far more to teach, and less time to spend with each student. ☐ **Philco-Ford's answer:** machines to help teachers communicate knowledge to the student at his own pace. ☐ Computerized teaching devices which allow a two-way dialogue between student and machine. ☐ The School District of Philadelphia has recently purchased a highly advanced Philco-Ford automated system for education, an important first in a burgeoning business with a billion dollar potential. ☐ Ford is solving problems in many other growth areas. In medicine. In space. In world nutrition. In microelectronics. ☐ Ford is where what's happening . . . happens.

THE WHITE · HAINES OPTICAL COMPANY

SOLD TO:

ADDRESS

BRANCH	ACCOUNT NO.	APP.	DATE

Salesman _____

Date _____

Written By _____

Dr Berry

	CODES			CUST. ORD. NO.	OUR ORD. NO.	INVOICE DATE	TERMS		INVOICE NO.
TRAN.	SALE	TERM					2% 10TH, NET 30TH	NET	

QUANTITY		PRODUCT CODE	CAT. NO. AND DESCRIPTION		UNIT PRICE	AMOUNT
ORDERED	B/O	SHIPPED				

1 — BriteSide Black Qual

1 " " WG Oct

1Kit — Bucto — Credit BriteSide Gold

	SUB TOTAL	SALES TAX	POSTAGE	TOTAL

DATE SHIPPED

FORM 1401 (REV. 2-72)

tpc Typographic Printing Co. — Cols., O.

Tell employees. Chrysler's massive corporate identity programme was introduced through the employee newspaper. Tunnel Cement used broadsheets for each employee, a brochure for shareholders, a synchronized news release to the Press, and a leaflet showing the new sack designs to foremen and workers on building sites.

A dynamic corporate identity programme was launched by Eastern Airlines which included design of offices, equipment, uniforms, and all other manifestations, including theme music for advertising. A record of it was given to all employees.

(a) Less than a year after it was introduced over 80 per cent of Swedish people correctly identified this new symbol for the Co-op.

(b) Albert Heijn, largest supermarket group in the Netherlands, replaced twenty or more ways of writing the company name with this one symbol and letterstyle. Because the symbol is seen virtually every day by every housewife, it was thought the design could be extremely simple. This has proved effective. After six months use, the symbol was identified correctly by 48 per cent of housewives interviewed in a research study.

Dutch Oil Company. Design by Total Design.

While variations to a basic identity can occasionally add to it in special circumstances, the greatest care should be exercised. These two examples, taken from design manuals, show how the good company restricts variation. The UniRoyal Manual includes this section on 'incorrect use' of the symbol. The manual of MacMillan Bloedel shows these examples of misuse with the introduction, 'It is imperative that the implementation of our corporate identification be rigidly controlled in terms of consistency. . . .'

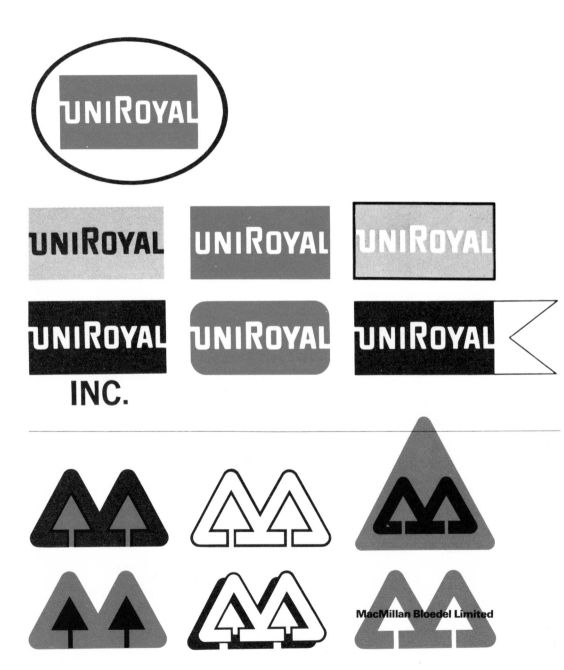

Group asked Interscan, a London company, to test new package designs for their crisps. The research was intended to cover three main areas: (a) general impressions conveyed by the new packaging; impressions of the manufacturer, the product, and people likely to form the prime market; (b) overall preference for the old or new packages; reasons for preference; (c) impressions of the logo in terms of the image conveyed.

The research report stated that:

> it was of special concern that a diagnosis could be made of the image conveyed; whether, for example, the manufacturer was projected as large, modern, efficient, hygienic and possibly a bit clinical and whether an impression of this kind is, in the minds of consumers, less effective than the 'fun' image which has for some time characterised a sector of the market.

This particular question expresses a dilemma. While the company wanted to see whether the new image was broadly right, they did want guidance on this subtle point. The answer could obviously influence their promotion behaviour significantly.

This test was carried out very quickly. A sample of 150 children, teenagers, and young mothers, selected by sex, age, and class, were interviewed in London and Southampton. Interestingly the tests were conducted with the aid of colour slides of various old and new packages with and without the brand name, and of the logo in isolation.

The results were clear. One of the new packages was preferred by 80 per cent of the people interviewed; another by 71 per cent. Shown an unbranded new package, 92 per cent thought they would like the crisps. Asked about the company, 58 per cent of the people interviewed thought the company was 'good', 'large', 'hygienic', 'clean', 'modern', and 'go-ahead'. A mere 2 per cent thought the firm conservative. Eighty-four per cent said 'yes' when shown the unbranded new packet and asked whether they would say that it was a good firm or not.

Smiths Food Group were particularly anxious to shift their image and their appeal from older to younger people. They were satisfied when research showed that the packaging would be thought likely to appeal to children (70 per cent of respondents said this), teenagers, and young mothers. Thus, the difficult question was answered. The research company felt able to report:

> It can be suggested with some confidence that far from detracting from the appeal to younger people, the new pack, with its image of modernity, hygiene and efficiency combined with colourfulness, has also successfully acquired a young look.

A series of questions sought to discover the kind of people likely to buy the crisps. A consistent pattern emerged: people would have a sense of humour (68 per cent); be happy-go-lucky (76 per cent); fashionable (79 per cent); gay (81 per cent); an 'ordinary' person (82 per cent); and would care about cleanliness (84 per cent). Interscan sum this up pithily by describing the new Smiths audience as 'young, swinging but basically conventional'.

The value of this information to the company is obvious. Throughout this research it was impressive how strongly people felt able to comment on the company by looking at the packaging: a point neglected by many manufacturers. See the figures in this particular test. Ninety-one per cent of the respondents said the company was a modern/quite modern firm; 67 per cent said it was large and efficient; 96 per cent said it was a hygiene-conscious/fairly hygiene-conscious firm. Equally decisive results were achieved in scales covering product attributes. Fresh/fairly fresh was chosen by 95 per cent. Ninety-two per cent thought the product would be high quality.

At the least, such results confirm that the basic image objectives had been accomplished. The company may project itself with confidence knowing that the basic material it is using is doing what they want it to do. Not all companies can be so sure.

An important reason for using market research, of course, is not only to see whether the corporate identity is doing what it is supposed to do, but to try to pinpoint areas for executive judgement. Research can indicate areas for design change.

The example of Smiths Food Group was interesting because a dramatic change was thought necessary, and was accomplished. Perhaps more often the problem is less sharply defined. A company with a strong, satisfactory identity may find itself moving slightly out of date, or at least be aware that in a few years' time its image will become dated.

The experience of a foot care firm is an example. Large, successful, and specialized, this company has become a household name in many countries. Its basic products tend to be purchased by older women. But the company saw the need to attract younger audiences and to keep its communication with existing customers up to date. It needed a shift in emphasis. Design consultants were appointed. A statement of the communication goal and a detailed brief were arrived at. Design changes were recommended, including some policy recommendations of a complex and fundamental nature. The basic design interest focused on packaging, and these were tested to determine attitudes to product and company alike. Research was carried out among 902 women in three cities. Recruiting was done on a quota basis to ensure that the sample represented the total female population. In a systematic way they were shown the old packages and variations of new packages. Each type of package test was rotated so that what the researchers call 'fatigue' was evenly spread. The test was extremely thorough. Certain findings are of relevance here. First, the shift in emphasis was seen to have been accomplished. The new designs were associated with the younger, better off, better educated, more sophisticated woman. Though the *proportion* altered significantly, the image remained acceptable to existing audiences and, indeed, was preferred by them. This clear but unfrightening shift was also evident when the research showed that while current users of foot products preferred the new packaging, the numbers of non-users that now accepted it increased markedly.

This augured well for the company's endeavours to attract new customers. Eighty-eight per cent of all women interviewed preferred the new packaging. Page after page of detailed analysis of attitudes to specific products revealed the same broad shift.

The following figures give a remarkable indication of the degree of image movement. The number of respondents who thought the *old* packaging would appeal to older women was 68 per cent. When shown the *new* packaging this dropped to 52 per cent. The number who thought the *old* packaging would appeal to the traditionally minded was 52 per cent. When shown the *new* packaging this dropped to 42 per cent. Conversely, the shift of people who thought the packaging would appeal to younger people went up from 13 to 26 per cent; up-to-date people, up from 39 to 50 per cent. This was not brought about by making only slight changes. The packages were fundamentally redesigned to accomplish important practical changes. A primary purpose of the research was to determine whether these changes could be brought into effect without damage to existing customer relationships. The results suggest that, if carefully handled, it is possible to control and shift a corporate image of a company to the extent required, and to do this while making fairly radical packaging changes.

We have seen some ways research can aid design decision, and can check whether a scheme is broadly right and if there are danger areas to avoid. Just as corporate communications is a continuous process, so should the checkback process be continuous: perhaps once a year is the right frequency, just to make sure that the corporate identity is accomplishing the required goals. There is an obvious reason: the situation in which any organization finds itself is constantly changing. New competitive developments, changes in tax laws, shifts in attitude to industry or to particular nations, even the impact of a single event, can alter attitudes to the organization.

The key to all research effort lies in defining clearly the problems one wants solved. From this, competent judges will be able to select the right research method to use and be able to pick the right company to do the work. This is particularly necessary not only in the interests of economy but even more of efficiency. People trust figures. If these figures are laid out in neat tables (and have been paid for) they will be trusted more. Therefore, it is important to make sure that the suppliers of such trusted information are themselves competent and experienced in the research technique thought best.

When the objective has been defined, the technique selected, the research company chosen, the work can start. It is necessary to allow both sufficient time and money for a research exercise. Often client companies and designers underrate the time factor, and ask the research company to act faster and more superficially than they would choose to do. The risks are obvious: you can't take an aeroplane ticket three-quarters of the way to New York – you end in the sea. The same can be said for market research.

When results are available, it is necessary for the client company and designers to analyse them carefully. Then they should confirm their conclusions with the research company to make sure such conclusions can be drawn on the basis of the figures presented.

Responsibility should remain with the executive of the client organization who should be prepared to provide the guidance designers need.

What to look for in a corporate identity presentation

It is wrong to take the view that because it is the *quality* of work that counts the *presentation* by the designer to the client is unimportant. Anyone who ever worked in this field has seen perfectly valid design schemes fail because the presentation went wrong. And that is wasteful.

This is no argument for false persuasion. It is most important that people receiving the presentation of a new corporate identity should have the underlying implications drawn to their attention. If there are thorny political areas, they should not be glossed over. It is only honest to make it clear to people what they are being asked to accept. It's also common sense. If problems arise later that were not envisaged when the scheme was agreed, trouble is inevitable.

The purpose of this chapter, therefore, is to suggest to client companies what they should look for in a presentation of corporate identity recommendations; how they should judge what they see.

Because the company is taking long-term decisions, often of greater importance than it realizes, every effort should be made to cast the presentation in a serious light. It should be formal and businesslike. All the effective decision-makers should be present. Responsible company executives and designers alike, should be thoroughly prepared. They should be sure of all the arrangements, prepare a clear agenda, predict possible questions, prepare and distribute summaries, have specific questions for decision ready, know what succeeding steps will be.

Earlier, we saw the need to have a 'design platform' agreed by client and designer alike before creative design began. The purpose was to define the objective of design activity. This document should be available at the design presentation, and should provide the criteria for judging what is presented. The question for the board to consider is, not 'Do we *like* this scheme?' but, 'Does this scheme meet the objectives we agreed originally?'

The format of a presentation must vary to suit the audience, the complexity of the problem solved, and the budget. Sometimes the number of people present creates other problems. Thirty people attended the British Rail presentation. When the members of one board of a Company visited the designer for a design presentation they had between them 'more bowler hats than my secretary could carry'. But whatever the size there will always be certain basics. First, a summary of the client's brief: what has he asked the designer to do? Second, a résumé of the problem. Third, an analysis of the steps taken by the designers to solve it, including reference to the agreed design platform. Fourth, the proposed solution. Fifth, a summary of the proposed solution in relation to the criteria in the design platform. Sixth, an outline of the recommended next steps. Seventh, specific questions for decision.

The client should always want to know how the design was arrived at; why this design is proposed; how it compares with competitors; how it works in action. To convey this information, the designers should show and the client wish to see the ingredients: how the design was built up; how it compares with other successful marks, related or not; and the designers' own process of development and elimination. Designers should show and clients expect to see the identity as it may appear in use in a competitive environment.

These illustrations of practical use should be as natural and as specific as possible. For example, if the company goes in for exhibitions, then it should be shown a redesigned exhibition stand. With imagination, it is possible to show a variety of applications. The designers should remember that, although vital, up to now it has all been theory. This is the practical part as far as the client is concerned. Often this part of the presentation opens clients' eyes to potential benefits more convincingly than reports will ever do.

The presentation given by a consultant design team to General Biscuits near Antwerp was typical. Given on slides, it recounted the background, then showed how the company could look to the passing motorist seeing a directional sign, to the visitor seeing the nameplate on the office doors, on the uniform of a receptionist, and on the matchbook of an employee; to the wholesaler seeing a liveried driver and his bright, newly painted vehicle, and the group mark on a shipping case; and to the consumer seeing packaging and reading newspaper advertising. From any vantage-point, the company looked the same. This slide sequence was created carefully but economically.

The presentation given to British Rail was extremely thorough. It included a slide presentation with taped commentary, a report on design policy, and an exhibition with, among other things, complete uniforms of railway staff (based on visits to nine countries and details of the clothing regulations of them all); it included large models of rolling stock and engines, an actual interior of part of a train.

The presentation given to the Koninklijke Zout Organon, a huge Dutch combine, had to be flexible and portable because the chairman was travelling a great deal at that time and little or no notice of his availability was possible. Even so, it included examples of their proposed new identity on a ship, worked in metal on a building sign, on a recruitment advertisement, an annual report, on packaging, on lorries, an exhibition stand.

All this may sound excessive. But it is necessary for the client to be assured that any scheme suggested will work in practice. Also, it provides the designers with practical opportunities to work out potential problems.

Twyfords, is a sanitaryware manufacturer based in Stoke-on-Trent, traditional centre of English pottery and china. Any design they adopted had to be capable of being stencilled and fired onto ceramic washbasins. The designer, Geoffrey Gibbons, had to discover the technical limitations this imposed, and design accordingly. He also had to demonstrate to the managing director and technical staff that his solution worked.

An example of the thoroughness involved in a good presentation occurred when their new corporate identity was presented to Albert Heijn, the Dutch supermarket chain. The executives seeing the presentation raised two doubts. First, the spacing of the name was questioned. This was one of the first uses of a new typeface called Brasilia, designed by Professor Hollenstein in Paris. The designers were able to answer the questions by tabling a letter from Professor Hollenstein applauding their specific use of his type. The second query concerned the colour recommended for vehicles: there was a fear it would fade. The designers were able to name local paint suppliers who could provide the correct colour to the company's specification.

In truth, there is no substitute for this kind of thoroughness, as Albert Heijn had already learnt. They had previously employed a foreign designer. His main recommendation was a symbol shaped like a Q for quality. The trouble was that in Dutch 'quality' is spelt with a K (*kwaliteit*).

This, one hastens to say, is an extreme example. But, in a dramatic way, the dangers of superficiality are underlined. Less colourful errors can still be costly. The board needs to question carefully.

While we are thinking here primarily of seeing the presentation of the visual identity of the organization, the total personality of the organization is an influence. Thus, whatever is proposed should have implications for all manifestations and activities of the organization. The board should recognize this. Architecture, advertising, public relations, brand policies may well come into the main presentation.

There is no reason why standard instructional techniques should not apply to presentations: variety, appeals to the maximum number of senses, and audience participation. To accomplish the first, the design organization can use the spoken word, the written word, film, slides, flip charts, designs on boards, and models, and create applications to hold in the hand.

André Tassier, in Brussels, once charmed the cigar-smoking president of a large company by offering him a light from a book of matches with his proposed new identity on them. Another company, having seen a slide presentation, were given key rings and a patch of carpet and packages, all identified in the proposed new style, to hold and judge.

Overdone, this could descend to gimmickry. But there is a line above that which says that subconsciously people are helped to judge things if they can touch and move them.

When they were presented ideas for a new visual identity, Storstockholms Localtrafik, Stockholm's local public transport system, were shown slides explaining the problem and recommended solution; then they were given samples of printed and typed letters, then shown a uniform hat, a model bus, a patch of carpet with the identity woven into it, and finally a display on board showing the essential decisions to take.

The chairman should ask the designers what decisions are required and, importantly, what happens next. Both questions sound basic, but are often forgotten. One has seen board members troop out of a meeting without any real curiosity about the implications and cost of what they have seen.

There is room in a good presentation for imagination, without losing seriousness. In advertising circles this is common and may be expected. When Kingsley, Manton, & Palmer, the London agency, made a presentation to Regent Oil Company, they dramatized the need for decision effectively. Esso's 'Put a Tiger in your Tank' campaign was at its height. KMP interspersed their presentation with reminders of the competition. Many similar stories could be told. Such excitement has so far escaped designers who tend to treat their presentations weightily. Doubtless in this respect agencies and designers will move closer together in the future.

It may be said that the companies used to receiving slick advertising presentations are accustomed to judging creative presentation. For companies without this frequent experience, care is necessary.

What sometimes happens is that the big presentation is planned so carefully, like a theatrical production, that its creators forget the point, that is to help the client company make the proper decisions. A way to do this is to clarify and spell out what these decisions are, then ask for them. This is a genuine service to people who are seeing a lot of new material, outside their usual field, for the first time. They could be forgiven for not knowing immediately the key points to settle.

Again, it is important to underline the implications of the decisions asked for. Changes of policy may well be involved and, if so, these should be made clear.

It is essential for the designers to get approval to continue the direction of work. It is remarkable how vague people can become at this moment. While they may have a broad view and even a general plan agreed earlier, it is

In any large organization the need for design coordination is felt. When a consultant designer was appointed to the Post Office one of his first jobs was to find responsibilities for design. Twenty-one departments were involved in the design of kiosks. These were different from those responsible for letterboxes, seen in the same streets. This chart shows the mess, and F H K Henrion's proposals.

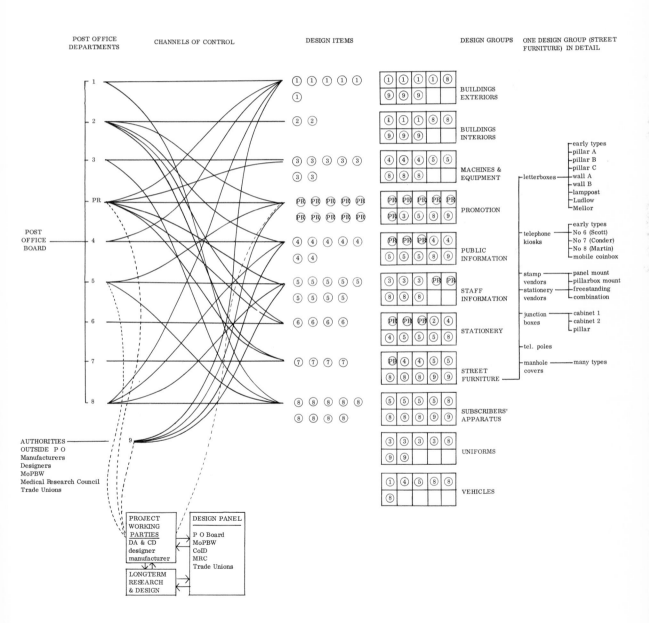

desirable that a precise and costed programme for the next phases should be available for the client to assess. This programme must be related practically to the specific situation. Client and designer must know what they are working to. A number of questions for decision arise at this point which influence immediate action. For example, is the suggested identity to be researched? Is it to be shown to other people before a final decision is taken? Is it to be introduced quickly or will it be introduced when a large number of applications are available? Will the introduction be timed to fit in with a special time or event? Will the changeover be immediate, or will things be changed only as stocks run down or replacement is necessary?

The designers making the presentation should be expected to have recommendations ready for all these questions, and to have at least rough cost estimates. Client companies should look for such information.

Maybe an implication of this is that the people receiving the presentation should be ready for it. General experience suggests that this is rarely the case. Successful design work is a dialogue between client on one hand, design group on the other. Dean McKay, vice-president of IBM in New York, has pointed out that:

Quality design demands at least two things: talented designers and a client that appreciates their work.

If a presentation is made in that climate of understanding it will be successful.

On the client's side, it is only fair for a chairman to identify and acknowledge the areas of expertise at such presentations. One sees errors committed in the name of democracy or concensus, or a quiet life. Just as the chairman would be wise to understand where the experienced judgement of certain individuals on his board is valuable and relevant, so he should recognize the limitations. It is by no means uncommon to see the opinions of designers ignored or overruled in just the areas where they are strongest and for which they have been retained.

Eastern Airlines, André Kostelanetz, and the Girl from Ipanema

The Soaring Spirit of the new Eastern – the lyrical beauty of an aircraft in flight – the exalted triumph of man's Conquest of the Skies – all these have been joyously captured in the melodies of the record.

This blurb appears on the sleeve of a record issued by an airline to its 19,000 employees in the United States as part of a programme to introduce a new corporate identity. The singer, mostly swamped by Soaring Strings, is Astrud Gilberto, the Brazilian girl who made her name with 'The Girl from Ipanema'. The first song, we read, is the 'Fly Eastern' theme.

This clean, free, lyrical statement of the joys of flying captures the need of the whisperjet in flight. Designed to be used with beauty shots of the plane in the skies, it features big unison strings in a soaring melody, supported by a counter point of French horns that evoke the feeling of open air!

The blurb goes on in similar vein, not, it appears, unsuccessfully. A news flash reported that the New York Philharmonic Orchestra, under André Kostelanetz is making a 12-inch LP of the *Music of Eastern* and this, too, will be distributed to employees.

(This success has since been scooped by TWA who bought rights to Jim Webb's 'Up, Up, and Away' pop song, have had half a million produced and in the summer of 1968 spent £7 million to make it a household refrain across Europe, Africa, and Asia.)

Every weapon in the armoury was used by Eastern to introduce their undoubtedly brilliant scheme. There's a new visual identity, packed into a large, but clear manual covering everything from aircraft liveries to baggage tags, VIP lounges to uniform badges, and how to write the hours of opening on a ticket-office door. There are new uniforms for hostesses, new ground services, a new slogan ('See how much better an airline can be'), new advertising in magazines, on TV, radio, and posters.

Examples and explanations of it all have been sent to employees not only to inform them (though this is better than most firms do) but to involve and enthuse them as well. Throughout the advertising, biggest in the airline's history, is an emphasis on people: crews, ground staff, reservation clerks, and behind-the-scenes staff whom passengers never meet. The emphasis is pointed out to employees in the explanations of the advertising. They are told the advertising makes a promise. 'How well we fulfill it,' says the explanation, 'is up to each of us at Eastern.' This makes a clear appeal to the staff to help project the airline favourably.

'What's behind Eastern's New Look?' they are asked on the folder containing the material sent them. 'It's *you*.' While in print this may seem strained, the effect of the material, with good copy, graphics, and photography, and the thoughtfulness running through it, make a striking impression. It illustrates a dynamic role of corporate identity introduction: not only to inform but also to unite company personnel. In Eastern's case this is taken further, to invite the wholehearted support and cooperation of the staff.

An important implication is that the airline genuinely wants to change and is changing. The corporate identity work is not thought of as a bright paint that will cheer up and preserve a crumbling edifice. The change comes from within, and is made obvious by design. Indeed, this is the Eastern story. A new president took an ailing airline, losing money, with little stronger than the passengers' WHEAL club (*We Hate Eastern Airlines*), and in two years improved its service and sales to the extent of substantial profits and becoming one of the biggest lines in America.

Serious designers, like serious management, recognize the wisdom of this approach. The director of graphics at Allied International Designers in London is always careful to probe the true spirit of a company before embarking on an identity programme.

A manufacturer of floor cleaning and maintenance equipment approached a London design house to get a corporate identity programme under way. Having taken a look at the company, the designers decided that what it needed first was a clear marketing plan. Consultants were appointed and it was only after eighteen months that the designers felt they had something to go on.

The need to make people aware of genuine change was a main reason for British Rail's new corporate identity programme. (Because this case is one of the largest and best of its kind, it keeps occurring in this book.) Proposals for a new look at the way the railways projected themselves were presented to the advisory committee with the words:

> The prime reason for the adoption of a corporate image for British Railways lies in its commercial value. British Railways needs a new look to stimulate a new faith in the national service it performs and *to draw attention to the many improvements now in the course of development.* . . . [Author's italics.]

Indeed, it was only when Dr (now Lord) Beeching was brought in to run the railways, from being deputy chairman of ICI, and when he immediately injected realistic commercial management into the sprawling nationalized system, that design started getting anywhere. When he introduced the new corporate identity and design policy to the public in 1965, he said:

> The railways corporate identity programme is the visible expression of the great managerial effort which has been introduced into the railways in recent times. It is intended to emphasize visually our progress towards a unified, efficient and viable railway system.

Again, we see design being used to tell and emphasize, but not to substitute for, the truth.

As we saw earlier, a practical goal for communication of this kind is to accelerate the shift to more favourable characteristics. It is possible to hope and believe that widespread use of the new identity by the railways has helped to raise their standards of management and service even though political upheavals have disrupted continuity of leadership and purpose. Many companies claim that new design policies can increase confidence in the organization and create a climate receptive to change because the change is made clear.

It would be under-utilizing a new corporate identity to neglect its promotion potential. Some people do. The second largest public company in its field in Europe embarked on such a scheme (the outward manifestation of thrusting new management). It is typical of many. Having arrived at a new design policy in a model way, it then allocated in its first year about one-tenth of the sums it should have done. Although anxious to burst out of an old, inefficient image surrounding it, the company failed to register the reality of the new organization, either externally or internally, and will take years to do so. Not only have promotion, PR, and employee-relations opportunities been wasted, but the active role of corporate communication in helping to effect change has been neglected.

Forward-looking executives often see design as a useful instrument in their struggle to effect new organizational structures. It is a curious fact that a logical approach to the visual expression of a company sometimes reveals and makes clear inconsistencies in the organizational structure which may have passed unnoticed for years. Perhaps it is not surprising. The designers must understand an organization before they can deal with its communications. Their work will inevitably lead them to want to simplify the tangled jungle of interrelationships between product managers, departments, companies, and divisions that grow up within a group. Being new to it and impartial, designers can point out the logic of certain corporate links which sometimes lie hidden under the more obvious human relationships.

Although the design consultant is not a trained management consultant in the normal sense, the more he works within industry the more he learns about it. The more advanced design offices already have trained marketing men on their staff or as consultants to them. Even without these special skills, the modern designer has a good deal of experience of working within organizations of all kinds.

Stuart Rose, a designer notable for his eloquence no less than his judgement, talked once about the modern design office.

> People come to a design office now expecting to find skills or an understanding of the expertise they want.

In order to do his own job properly, the designer sometimes feels it necessary to ask why the organization he sees in the better firms is not used in those less advanced. This is particularly so in the case of design and corporate communications. Because the whole subject is relatively new only a few firms have really come to grips with it. The establishment of 'offices of corporate communication', seen in American companies, is virtually unheard of in Europe. From experience, the designer has learnt the need for a central unifying organization for all the manifestations of corporate personality. He is likely to recommend such a structure.

Regrettably, only a handful of even the largest organizations have such an organization. Still fewer have attempted to link verbal expressions with visual ones. In modern conditions this absurdity cannot continue. In part it is traceable, directly, to the organization structure existing in industry today. PR, advertising, design, employee relations, architecture, vehicle fleets, and the rest are seen too often as unrelated and, apart from advertising, insignificant parts of corporate activity. Things will change. It won't be long before companies appoint a director of communications, whose task will be to weld these now diverse strands together into one consistent expression of the organization.

Designers have been called 'the trained dreamers of industry'. One of the implications of this is that they are perpetually casting their minds forward. Problems they deal with today will show results some time in the future. They must think of the future and, while not neglecting the realities of the moment, help companies position themselves correctly for the future. To some degree, this bears on the view they have of corporate activity and corporate organization. If, for example, the futurist designer believes that information processing will become a major factor in business, he is likely to be impatient with an organization that lacks a librarian. If he sees that the relationship between manufacturing and marketing has already changed totally in the last twenty years, he will see that his own design work can only be of limited benefit to a company that is still dominated by engineers. As a 'trained dreamer of industry' the designer should not be prevented from making comments which appear to be beyond his domain. Indeed, he may need to if his work is to be of real value.

Two likely prognostications are relevant. First, it is extremely likely that good communications will become increasingly important to industry. The disjointed functions in industry of promotion and publicity today will almost certainly be replaced by a stronger, richer communication team with an influence far greater than any departments can exert now. Second, as industry becomes more sophisticated, management will tend to 'rent' the skills it needs more, even, than it does today. Consultants will grow in number, and stature. But they, too, will need coordinating. A possible solution lies, once more, in recognizing the central value of a statement of corporate communication goals. In time one would hope to see one main brief prepared which states the overriding purpose of the corporation, and give the facts commonly needed by any consultant. It would have appendixes for the specialist functions under review.

This comment springs from a belief in the interrelation and interdependence of all corporate activities. Just as a company's communication cannot be isolated from its product range, nor can either be divorced from production capability or financial resources. Today, when the elements are integrated to accomplish common goals (still astonishingly rarely), they are linked under the banner of marketing. And because this means satisfying the demands of the market, it is axiomatic that manufacturers should find out what the market requires and use what means of communication that exist to satisfy this demand. Thus communications, at best, are used to support products. In time one would expect this relationship to alter. Good two-way communications will have a wider, more pervasive role. By the *input* of information from the market, industry will be able to shape its policies and determine its product range, to suit the market. By *output* of information, it will be able to appeal to the market in appropriate terms and so help create an acceptable environment for its products to fill. Companies most sensitive to changing market needs will be in a better position to meet them. See it the other way around: the customer, bewildered by choice, will respond to the companies that are most obviously in tune with his needs.

Ironically, the products that flow from these companies will be one, but only one, of the criteria by which companies are judged. It will be entirely possible for firms to offer perfectly satisfactory products or services in themselves which do not succeed because the communication mechanism is inadequate or inappropriate. Perhaps one already sees signs of this.

Paul Foley, at one time chairman of the advertising firm McCann-Erickson said:

In this business you must have a much larger share of the mind than you have share of the market. And you must constantly, positively, keep building that share of mind.

It is logical to expect that, before long, companies in Europe, the United States, Japan, and elsewhere will establish at board level a director of corporate communications. Whether he will be responsible for the input of information as well as its output is unclear, though there are obvious points in its favour. The relationship between him and the marketing director also needs to be worked out.

Uncertain as this is, it is already clear that traditional and even current job descriptions and corporate hierarchies are in for a change.

Aided by his marketing director and director of corporate communications, the managing director will have the task of defining the basic corporate goals and laying down long-range objectives. These will be regularly reviewed and refined. Instead of the *ad hoc*, on-off research that currently goes on as new products are explored and developed, one will expect continuing research into the market. One purpose will be to watch its changes, another will be to check the company's own pulse.

One sees occasional examples of research used this way. Albert Heijn in the Netherlands, Chase Manhattan in the United States, the Co-operative movement in Sweden, Charrington United Breweries in the UK are among them, and there are others. But, apart from Chase Manhattan which has reviewed its position annually for five years, even these have been short-term image studies. The majority of firms don't bother at all.

It is also remarkable how few organizations have long-range planning units with a brief wide enough to review future developments in a broad way. Those that exist very often spend their lives poring over projections of growth in their existing product fields. Few are charged with the responsibility for being alive to changing patterns of social behaviour, which may well be influenced by political, scientific, and humanistic developments outside the limited sphere of study allowed to the forward planning unit.

Among successful executives in Britain today is Raymond Hudson, formerly managing director of Formica Limited. With as realistic an eye as anyone on current performance (during his four-year term of office, Formica's profits increased 30 per cent despite an enormous increase in world production capacity and tough price competition), he combines a sharp awareness of the need for innovation and change. Within one month of being appointed managing director of Potterton International (the heating equipment firm in the same De La Rue group), he had oriented the company totally towards marketing, set up a forward planning unit, asked it for five-year product and profitability goals and sketched ten-year targets, changing the long-held philosophy of the company. He said:

This central team will work on an international basis . . . from this source I expect to be told how to turn 'heating' into 'climate' as our development theme and eventual product range.

It is obvious that in today's rapidly shifting environment many companies will need to reassess their accepted attitudes in much the same way.

To restrict one's communication to sales conferences, the occasional product plug in the trade press, and existing product advertising is to reduce the chance of a dynamic thrust into new markets.

Corporate communications, therefore, must be bound integrally to corporate goals. And corporate goals, one may expect, may well be influenced by what can realistically be accomplished by communications. Peter Drucker believes that two essential functions for any firm now are marketing and innovation. Both of these depend on effective communications. For example, one may find corporate progress limited by an unsatisfactory input of market information. Or one could develop a product or service in tune with accurately predicted needs, but be unable to profit from it because the idea couldn't be understood or accepted sufficiently widely. It is even possible to imagine circumstances in which a company may develop a new product, have it accepted, but still fail to persuade people that the firm concerned is capable of producing good products in that field.

Public relations, employee relations, advertising, design of products, packaging exhibitions, print matter, uniforms, architecture and office planning, signage, dealings with the trade, suppliers, and city alike should be considered on two levels. First, for their immediate purpose. Second, for the influence they may have on shaping attitudes to the company.

Whether people acknowledge this or not, such coordination is extremely rare. IBM is a model to look at. Their annual report says the same things at a subconscious level as the company's products – excellently designed in human as well as functional terms. Both convey the same impressions as their architecture. Consistently excellent, forward looking and human, few firms have done more to probe the future and to relate man to it happily than IBM. They could not have achieved the success they have without good products. But can one disregard the dynamic role effective communications have played in their growth of the design part of all this? Their chairman has said: 'We think every nickel that we have put into design has paid off in IBM, and more.'

Three time scales exist, it seems, in which the combined forces of communication within a company can be effective. The first one is to make change apparent. The Eastern example, already quoted, is representative. If the ground is chosen carefully, and if the company uses the resources available, attitudes to an organization can be shifted. A press release won't go far. A few pictures in the trade journals won't alter long-held opinions. But a sustained and systematic campaign expressed through the company's staff, and through all available channels can come to people's attention and be accepted by them. What often happens is that companies alter their visual identity and nothing else. So, not only is the design unlikely to work fully, it is often in contradiction to all the other media which remain untouched. Not the least reason for insisting on coordinating all channels of communication is to make sure that one does not work against another. The thing is to recognize both the enormity of the task of changing attitudes and the opportunities presented by fully integrated communication effort. There is the strongest case for criticizing the parsimony and internal organizations which often prevent potentially good schemes from being promoted effectively. There are situations in which it is best to move quietly, but these are few. And that is still no argument for allowing the various channels of communication to operate independently and without relation to the main goal.

The second time scale is the short-term one: to support existing products or services. Again, it is essential to coordinate the diverse verbal and visual opportunities for promotion. While efforts are made, often at a product promotion level they are infrequently related to the long-term corporate position. Products come and go. Services alter out of recognition. Markets change. But the corporation, grow or merge as it may, is a continuing organism. It is necessary that nothing is done in image or in other terms to damage the corporate reputation. A criterion, therefore, for any product promotion must be the effect it may have on the company's position of respect. Put more positively, one of the criteria by which products will be chosen (and to some extent always have been subconsciously) is the influence they have on the corporate image.

This leads to the third time scale: the long-term one. We've seen the importance of plotting a course, of seeing a position for a company some years forward, and working towards it. This demands a long, forward look. And it means shifting purposefully the posture of an organization of any kind away from its present one towards something relatively few people in the organization will recognize the need for. This dynamic is essential but difficult to sustain. It means that corporate communication goals must be expressed in simple terms everyone can follow and be distributed to everyone involved. Second, performance should be regularly 'policed'. The office of corporate communications should review all outpourings (talks to the local Rotary, employee newspapers, and switchboard responses no less than plans for new offices and advertising campaigns) to make sure the stated goal is adhered to. To turn theory into practice, it is necessary to keep this long-term goal in mind always, for the future is built from today's actions. A number of successful organizations are moving this way. In the American cases we've seen, the director of corporate – or visual – communications (the title varies) claims the responsibility for every visible manifestation of his company and wants to approve any variations to the standards.

In 1965, Chrysler who, since 1962, had a director of corporate identity, set up what they called 'a new administrative activity' to be run by the same man. The new office is now responsible for office utilization and location, decoration, furnishing, general-purpose office equipment, office supplies, and corporate identity. The centralization is there for all to see. British Rail not only has a design officer with these responsibilities but also a steering committee which meets monthly. On this committee sit the chief architect, chief publicity officer, chief PRO, the director of design, a design 'officer', the chief passenger development officer, the outside design consultants, and a secretary.

Tandy Halford & Mills, the London designers, are retained to police the design operations of Owen Owen, a chain of retail stores. 'This,' says Tandy, 'is essential for some years.' He believes the designer should do it. 'The danger is that unless the designer constantly watches, mistakes occur and get worse.' These designers, too, receive a proof of every new series of Bovril label that is printed, for the same reason. In theory everything bearing the corporate name should be seen by the designer.

A current example of the curious contradictions that can occur happened with the new Cunard liner. From the start it was intended to be something new; modern, powerful, fast, comfortable. The exterior shape makes this obvious. A team of designers was appointed to design interior accommodation to new standards of taste. New materials have been employed. New graphic designs have been used throughout. The company's offices have all been redesigned to put them in the modern leisure/travel business. The code-name, 'Q4', had the same new flavour. But when the great day came to launch the ship and name her, the Sovereign named the ship after herself, using her prerogative. The dichotomy, between modern ship and traditional name, may not damage sales. But there is undoubtedly a gap between the desired image projection and anything one may learn from the name.

The need to survey corporate performance in relation to the stated communication goals obviously affects both investment and marketing policy. So the future bears on the present.

What happens if there are short-term sales to be had by selling through discount houses, but this appears to be against the long-term goal? Or if there is business to be had now by marketing low-cost services when the company wants to be seen in the future as at the top of its field? Evidently this relationship between present and future must be resolved. This means that, if there are not to be unceasing rows between those responsible for this year's sales and others concerned with long-range image, both must be a party to the long-range goal.

Throughout this chapter, indeed this book, has run the theme that more penetrating work needs to be done on image projection. More resources should be used. Communication should be given a new position of strength in the corporate structure. Doesn't it all cost more? Yes it does, although having more sense of purpose and strengthening the effectiveness of what one does may lead to economies. The president of Westinghouse claims that since coordinating their design and corporate identity work they have:

> already realized substantial savings in the cost of graphics, in buildings and most of all, in products.

Looking ahead one may foresee the present non-stop escalation of advertising appropriations (what Walter Margulies has called 'the advertising overkill') to be directed more specifically than at present.

It is true that most other aspects of modern business also cost more than the old methods they supplant. Purposeful, planned, and coordinated communications are not just a marginally better way of doing something industry does already. They stand for little less than a new approach to industry's relations with society, and represent one of the new ways industry will need to develop and prosper in the future.

Case histories in corporate identity

The Chinese curse, 'may you live in interesting times', must surely have been laid on a twentieth-century banker.

Nonetheless, bankers are cautious people. They have to be. It is all the more interesting to see how they view the idea of corporate identity and what, if anything, they are doing about it.

Emphatically, from California to Clydeside, banking is embracing the corporate identity idea with a vigour never seen before. The lofty halls and granite walls of the traditional bank are crumbling before the new wave of mass affluence. Recognizing the radical change, the banks are now anxious to attract new savers, small savers, with an open friendliness that would have been frightening only a few years ago.

The degree of friendly service is increasing sharply. In West Germany now, as in Florida, you can get a loan by telephone. Banks are merging to meet competition and to provide the resources the world's great companies increasingly require. The traditional big five British banks merged to become the still bigger two banks; Barclays and Martins in one constellation, Westminster and National Provincial in the other. Lloyds remains a single entity. Even before the arrangements were complete they were considering their identities.

Further north, the National Commercial Bank of Scotland, Glyn Mills, Williams Deacon's Bank, and the Royal Bank of Scotland have merged. Within two months they appointed designers to consider their communication situation in terms of both present and future, and to create a new identity for them.

Universally, banks see their role changing swiftly. The public they serve, the services they provide, and the competition they face, all are changing. The foreign invasion of London is gathering pace (belying suspicions that her position as the centre of international trade is declining). Twenty-two US banks have set up in London, most of them in 1968. Recent arrivals from Switzerland and elsewhere bring the total number of foreign banks in London to over 100. The Bank of America has branches in Birmingham, Manchester, and Dublin as well as London.

On the Continent the banks, dealing in stocks and shares, often have a different role from their British colleagues. But here, too, foreign competition (including US mutual funds) as well as the opportunities of the Common Market and mass affluence, are causing a new look to be taken at the whole service, promotion, and image of banking.

But how to go about it? Any organization is presented with a choice of ways to distinguish itself from others. Banks are a good example. The obvious similarity of their 'product' and services highlights the choice open to them. Examining the possibilities, it appears that there are at least three approaches they could take.

First, they could make it clear to their customers and staff that they are a service organization in modern terms. They could attempt to be, and be seen by their customers as, more friendly, obliging, and efficient. Second, they could simply try to be known as good in their field. People know what banks do, at least broadly. If a bank could invest its image with the traditional virtues of banking and financial security, plus being good at its job, this could do. A third approach could be to become a personality among competitors: when they're all the same, this one is different.

Examples exist of banks trying each of these approaches. More often, perhaps, there is the temptation if not the need, to blend the lot; to be friendlier and efficient, and reliable and unique. Should it be impossible to accomplish everything, then plainly, priorities are needed. The criteria outlined can provide starting-points for assessing communication goals. In Canada, the Royal Bank and the Bank of Montreal are two who have developed sophisticated new images for themselves. These Canadian examples are interesting. The Royal Bank of Canada, a private bank, has traditionally used the royal coat of arms, often shown in gold against a deep-blue background. Parliament objected consistently at the inference that it was a national institution. Finally, as the Quebeçois gained more power their voice could be heard. In addition to this, the bank realized that the cold officialdom, formality, and inflexibility of being identified as a national institution was not doing them any good. Like so many financial institutions, too, they had from time to time used a picture of their head office building as a symbol of stability. But what happens, their consultants asked, when you move, or when the building is obviously old fashioned?

Instead of the formal, and, by implication, autocratic image being conveyed, by this concentration on the centre and on the royal coat of arms, the designers advocated a lighter approach, with more emphasis on local branches. (In Canada there is a branch office for every 3500 people.) They recommend a six-point programme: a timeless logotype, a more effective symbol, a better colour, eliminate the building and royal coat of arms as design elements, a format for implementation, and a priority list for action.

Another Canadian bank, the Bank of Montreal, went through a similar exercise to 'emphasize its progressive thinking and modern world-wide services'. Fittingly, the introduction of their new corporate identity coincided with their 150th anniversary and Canada's centennial year. They appointed an experienced design office (Stewart & Morrison in Toronto) as their consultants for the task. After due study, the designer, Hans Kleefeld, created a symbol which he believed signified 'strength and stability at first glance'. At the same time, a standard way of writing the bank's name was developed to replace a multitude of styles that had come into use during the bank's history. On top of that, a slogan was created: 'Canada's first bank.' Historically correct, it defined the bank's aspirations. The name was given to the colour chosen: 'First Bank Blue.'

They call these elements 'communication components'. How these elements were applied to the many and various manifestations is worth noting. The consultants established what they called a temporary design control point on location. A design coordinator from Stewart & Morrison was given a desk in the bank's head office to see the implementation through. Finally, a design manual was created to help bank personnel maintain the new standards. The whole scheme for the Bank of Montreal has an integrity and simplicity likely to last.

In Scotland, the Clydesdale Bank (360 branches) handled their award-winning corporate identity programme in a slightly different way. Their scheme, which won for them a Royal Society of Arts gold medal for design management, started in 1963 when they decided to change their name and 'stick their neck out of the cocoon of traditional banking'. At the time, Clydesdale was one of five Scottish banks with little discernible difference in their appearance. They wished to identify themselves with:

... the progressive business world of today, the new spirit in Scottish industry and the computer age.

The Woudhuysen Design Group was appointed to handle the project. After a series of meetings, they defined three important characteristics to be communicated: stability, precision, and progressiveness.

The first step was largely an exercise in O & M. The bank had some 2000 forms; almost a third were cut out. Then they did a pilot study on 24 items, including the main letterhead, to establish basic design standards for all documents. They adopted standard paper sizes, chose a typeface to be used for all printing (Monotype Univers, series 689 medium, wherever possible, printed text is Didot), laid down principles for the use of the typeface, and created a new symbol for the bank. Then the basic identity was applied to many things.

Partly because he thinks that 'no corporate identity will work if the company is badly organized', Woudhuysen insists on control in the design or client organization. 'Without good control you cannot deal with exceptions,' he says and adds wistfully, 'and life consists of exceptions.' In fact, control of design is one of the four benefits Clydesdale Bank say they have received from their corporate identity work.

First, they name the opportunity for increased profits through what in a production company would be sales. By creating a positive visual identity, the level of recognition and acceptance of the bank is raised, and they believe this will encourage more people to use their services. Second, they point to the internal relations benefits. The bank claims that the design programme 'develops cohesive effort and pride in the bank from the staff'. The third benefit Clydesdale mentions is the direct saving in production costs for items that lie within the scope of the corporate identity programme. Lastly, they feel that the rationalization of forms has led to improved clerking.

The three schemes we've looked at are all essentially graphic solutions to image problems. One wonders whether the actual services provided by the banks, or the function and appearance of their branches will alter much. And yet surely this is the beginning.

We've been looking at banks because they show that corporate identity activity is the concern of a wide range of corporate structures and is by no means confined to the big consumer-oriented manufacturing companies. To take two other examples, in Manchester, the Girls' Friendly Society, formed in 1840 to tackle the social problems of the time, recently retained Keith Murgatroyd, a graphic designer, to redesign its literature and visual identity to express the modern services it now offers. The same designer was employed by a theological college in Salisbury (its principal is the Rev. Harold Wilson) for much the same purpose.

Evidently a need is felt throughout the community for clearer communications and even, one dare say, better design. It is not insignificant that local government, not hitherto renowned for its enthusiasm for modern design, is now embarking on corporate identification work.

Because their problems are different from those of commercial concerns, it may be interesting to examine what they have attempted to do and how they have gone about it.

Local government has been part of the administrative system of England since Saxon times. In its present shape, it dates back to the nineteenth century. The occasion for the initiatives we'll describe arose when, in 1965, a new organization structure was formed to administer the 8 million people and 620 square miles of London. One of the Greater London Council's first steps was to reduce by amalgamation the 90 local authorities of various kinds to 32 borough councils. The City of London itself has a separate structure.

The Borough of Camden in inner North London was one of them. The

Borough of Lewisham, in South-east London, was another. Each serves about 250,000 people. Each needed to identify its property and services anew. Their normal procedure would have been to ask the College of Heralds to create a new coat of arms for them, and then to apply this to everything from building sites to dustcarts, from the Mayor's regalia to demands for taxes (rates). This is what other boroughs did. But quite separately and autonomously, both Camden and Lewisham realized that the boroughs have a good story to tell, and they needed a clear and positive identity to help tell it.

Research has shown that only a quarter of Londoners know what borough they live in: so there is a need to identify. The image of local government tends to be authoritarian, remote, and shabby. In view of their libraries, swimming-pools, parks, social services, and massive house-building programmes, this is less than just. There is a need for the other half of any corporate identity programme: to convey the right impressions about the organization.

The Borough of Camden asked Wolff, Olins, designers practising in the area, to work on this. Defining the problem, they designed a symbol (a pattern of eight interlocking hands) and a colour scheme. The symbol, explains Olins, represents the human, interrelated structure of local government: voting, working, giving, and receiving. The colour scheme, a warm orange with white, looks, he feels, sympathetic and friendly:

> It takes the charity out of the meals-on-wheels service, makes the entrance to clinics and libraries more inviting, helps turn the roadsweeper with his vivid handcart from a drab, anonymous figure into an amiable person with a helpful job.

Whether corporate identity work actually changes people is questionable, though improved employee relations, through a sense of identification and corporate purpose, are commonly given as among the benefits of such work. Camden has applied its new scheme wholeheartedly. It is impossible to be there two minutes without being aware of the constructive work its local government does.

The Borough of Lewisham, which undertook a similar exercise at about the same time, has 70 people on its main council. Ten are aldermen, 60 are councillors. Reporting to them are 10 chief officers each responsible for a department. Indeed, when the idea of a corporate identity was first discussed a few councillors were in favour, some were apathetic, some were against spending the ratepayers' money. The Town Clerk (the principal officer on a *primus inter pares* basis) discussed the question with four groups of designers. Then he was empowered to appoint one to conduct a survey in the newly defined borough to examine the present situation.

Peter Cree and Geoffrey Woollard of Allied International Designers moved around the borough for two months, then produced a report, with photographs that delved into every corner of the borough's activities. The need for action became obvious to everyone.

(a)

(b)

(c)

(d)

(e)

The communications of a big company are widespread. Simple symbols and smart typography are not enough for the differing needs of (a) shareholders in London; (b) a pensioner in Australia; (c) footballer Eusebio in a Portuguese soap ad; (d) a freelance jobber in Greece; (e) office staff in Watford; a few of Unilever's audiences. Among their excellent publications are 'Unilever International', and (f) a series for older school-children, notably different in style. Companies with famous 'brand' names and policies have often thought it unnecessary to bother much with their overall corporate expression. Now new pressures are causing a reassessment. It is significant that Unilever, the archetypal 'brand' company, should have undertaken a corporate identity study. Their new symbol is shown at (g).

(f)

(g)

It included not only detailed comments on the appearance of objects, but on the whole approach of the council to its public. It suggested that the name itself should concentrate on 'Borough of Lewisham' or 'London Borough of Lewisham', that other less sympathetic descriptions be dropped. It advocated much greater identification of borough property and work. One photograph showed the architectural department offices, hidden behind a small café: hardly appropriate, the report noted laconically, for architects serving an area the size of Coventry. It showed new houses being built and observed that nowhere was the borough identified as the principal, a fact to be proud of. The report criticized the wording on signs as negative and punitive. A decaying park sign read: 'Children Keep Out. No dogs allowed.' In fact the park was reserved for old people, and the sign might have done better to say so. Requests to respect their comfort might be more readily understood. Vehicle fleets were dismissed with the word 'scruffy'.

Conclusions drawn were that the borough hid itself excessively, and when it was apparent it was shown negatively.

The report and first design solutions were shown to the General Purposes Sub-committee of the Council. They agreed it in principle. Because one clear recommendation was consistency, they felt they lacked the authority to carry the work further without bringing in the main council. This was done. Even when it was agreed, the practical question arose of how to get the work done. The designers recommended an organization. First they suggested that a central liaison officer be appointed, responsible for administering the scheme: Arthur Taffs, the PRO, was asked to do this. Then they suggested that design proposals be submitted to him, after discussion with the appropriate chief officers. If the designers proposed something the chief officer didn't like then a sub-committee (appointed by the General Purposes Committee) would arbitrate. A monthly meeting with the liaison officer was arranged. plus others as necessary. Perhaps because the relationships and organization were laid down from the start, the need for arbitration never arose.

The design scheme (a coronet on a blue background) is, at the time of writing, in its second year of implementation. It is being handled on a replacement basis.

What did this local government authority learn from their experience? The PRO who has been most deeply involved, cites four lessons. First, he says, go into it with a goal and a clear purpose in mind. Corporate identity is not just redesigning the letterhead. Second, have a firm intention to carry it through. Third, recognizing the non-profit nature of government, he urges the wisdom of going through the work quickly. Fourth, once standards have been set, stick firmly to them. It is normal for departments to want to stress their title and relegate the corporate identity, but says Mr Taffs, it is important to stand out against departments wanting to bend the overall identity.

The degree of detail gone into in this case has been deliberately done not only, hopefully, to aid others, but also to indicate how the practical complexities of organizing this activity may be met. Unquestionably, many corporate identity projects fail for two main reasons: first, the study beforehand is insufficient and second, the organization to take decisions and to progress work is ineffective. If both are well thought out, coherent corporate identities can emerge from the most complicated organization.

This chapter has taken case histories from banking and local government to emphasize the universality of the corporate identity problem. The need to define and express a corporate personality is widely felt. The point is that organizations have personalities whether they do anything about them or not. These may be unseen, unheard, incoherent, messy, aggressive, or pleasant, old fashioned, or modern, and many other things besides. The task today is to fashion this personality as a constructive instrument of corporate policy.

In this context the words of Reinhold Bergler, German psychologist and authority of imagery, may be quoted. In his book, *Psychologie des Marken und Firmenbildes*, he writes:

> It is possible to speak about a firm's personality in a proper sense only if it has a unique and unmistakably sharp focus and a clear separation from similar firms.

10

How to organize and administer the follow through

Many promising corporate identity programmes fail because they are not followed through properly. This chapter will concern itself with the follow through: how to make it effective.

It is sometimes thought that once a designer has presented his design recommendations his work is done. In corporate identity work, this is rarely so. At this stage, in fact, the problems suddenly assume a reality and complexity that can frustrate the unwary. Indeed, it is unusual for a company to foresee the inevitable implications of a corporate identity programme – even though it has committed itself to one.

The stage at which designs are presented and approved is not the end, only the end of the beginning. If a company arrives at a statement of communication goal and designs (symbols, letterstyles, colour schemes, and so on) that are appropriate and acceptable, it has laid the foundations of a corporate identity. As in any structure meant to last, good foundations are important, but they are not enough by themselves. This architectural analogy is good because it makes clear the fact that, even with strong foundations, it is still all too possible to erect a bad building.

So we should ask: 'What makes a good "building"?' Then: 'How do you make sure you get it?'

A good corporate identity scheme is one that effectively uses every suitable manifestation of an organization to convey appropriate messages consistently. Assuming that the basic design provides the means to convey appropriate messages, the next task must be to convey them *consistently*. This is where the follow through becomes so important. A number of factors make it difficult – not the least is that almost all the forces and inertias in a large organization work against the powerful singleness of purpose that is necessary.

Until anyone starts to apply a corporate identity scheme, it is a theoretical and relatively inexpensive matter, nice to think about, and interesting to work on. When the decision is taken to adopt it, the problems alter. For one thing, a consistent identity programme intrudes on almost all departments of a company. It affects advertising, packaging, the design of buildings, exhibition stands, print matter, and signs, and even, to a considerable extent, areas of marketing judgement and product policy. It certainly has cost implications of interest to financial controllers; it can have legal aspects affecting mergers and acquisitions. It should be no surprise if many of the men responsible for these functions raise objections: almost always one is imposing new strictures on them and to some extent reducing their freedom of action. There will be instances of disagreement and genuine difficulty. Moreover, even if one accepts that there may be some losses in the interests of a general gain, it is obviously important to minimize the losses.

There is a big difference between asking people to accept a general idea and telling them to alter their communications with trade or public. But it is wrong to put off detailed change in the interests of harmony or to suit the natural conservatism of salesmen and others. So the problems of implementing a corporate identity become human, specific, and complex. Whoever is responsible for the scheme must fight to preserve the clear idea he started with – not giving *much* but knowing *where* to give.

Specific marketing and communication problems in the different departments of a firm must be faced, balancing the merits of practical 'here-and-now' activity with longer-term possibilities. These questions are not always easy to resolve in the best long-term interests of a company when the executives concerned are held accountable for short-term results. Many good corporate identity schemes founder on this rock. To ignore it, or to decide always in favour of the immediate selling situation, is to increase the chance of failure.

Immediate marketing requirements should not be ignored or overruled, but such problems may arise and must be reckoned with. They can occur at almost any level. It is likely that the main problems will have been foreseen and recommendations made by the designers. But this may not be true of all situations in a large company. New decisions may be required. It sometimes happens that policies agreed by the board are not endorsed by executives who have to carry them out, and whose point of view and loyalty is more restricted.

Clearly, the board of the corporation must state its long-term ambition and must give someone the authority to arbitrate in favour of the long-term, overall good.

Another practical problem of follow through sounds pedestrian, but may assume large proportions. This is the question: 'Who pays for it?' The trap is that most of the items that need to be redesigned come within someone's budget already. It is easy to think that the cost of implementing a corporate identity scheme is slight because most of the expense must be incurred anyway. While this is true, it leads to two difficulties: there are a number of jobs to be done for which there is no budget, and at least some of the expense needed is additional to normal requirement. It is usual to see department heads expected to make major conversions within the budget allowed for daily trading. This imposes impossible strains. It means the change can't take place at the proper rate, and encourages the executive to find cheaper sources of supply. This may lead to a lowering of quality that is directly contrary to corporate aims. Indeed, because the value of corporate communications has not been recognized, the chances are that the company is not spending enough on its visible manifestations anyway. The other practical difficulty is that, if all the cost of change must come from existing budgets, the whole speed and quality of implementation is cast into the hands of the people who control the budgets: people who are more likely to have sectional interests than global ones.

It is optimistic, both in organizational and financial terms, to hope that a corporate identity scheme can be put through properly with existing budgets. It is necessary to establish separate budgets both to pay for the rate, thoroughness, and quality of change that is required, and to pay for the extra load demanded of departmental budgets.

This is a vital point. Understanding by the board of the need for a positive extra commitment and recognition of the scale of expenditure involved, is essential to the success of a corporate identity programme.

It is astonishing how few companies are prepared to make what should be thought of as capital investments in a new corporate identity. Frequently they expect to create a whole new personality for the company without any extraordinary expenditure. Squeezing budgets here, waiting there, doing it on the cheap somewhere else, the results they achieve are often as imperfect as one might predict.

Time is an important factor. It is possible to lower expenditure substantially by changing over from old design to new only when old stocks run out, or things need replacement. While on occasions it is right to take advantage of this economical method, it is wrong to think that nothing more is required. On this basis some manifestations wouldn't change for thirty years. The Netherlands Railway paint their locomotives every eight years. Having adopted a new design scheme, handling it on a replacement basis the change-over could take eight years. It is important to establish a momentum of change which can be varied but should be faster than natural wastage would permit. This means that the budget allowed for corporate identity work must be greater than the normal sums allowed for the activities it embraces.

So far we have covered three essentials for successful implementation. First, to recognize the scale of change (the basic design scheme is not the end, but the beginning). Second, to be prepared to adhere to the initial clear communication concepts for the organization in the face of local argument. Third, to allocate sufficient funds to give the work a proper chance.

There are more requirements. The board must appoint a senior executive to carry through the scheme. He must have the authority to move about the organization freely and to impose a consistent scheme on the diverse departments involved. The need for this executive to have the power to maintain a clear line is evident enough when one thinks of the forces of economy, expediency, and independence against which he has to struggle.

Peter Cree, who, at Allied International Designers, has controlled such design projects for Albright & Wilson, Meredith & Drew, the Royal Bank of Scotland, and others, believes that success in implementation:

> . . . depends much on having the experience, knowledge and number of people needed in the design organization; and also in the experience and authority to *persuade the client to establish an effective organization himself.*

Every successful scheme has such a man behind it. The weaker his authority, the weaker the scheme will surely be. Although committees are often necessary it is still true that one man should bear real responsibility. British Rail operates through a committee. So does the John Lewis Partnership, as we saw. It is best if the committee acts in an advisory way to the executive responsible. Some companies have a specially set up organization to handle their corporate identity, but this is extremely rare. Shell International has a manager of 'visible manifestations'. Chrysler and General Mills have a head of corporate identity, each with departments under him. Sometimes the chief marketing executive (Smiths Food Group, Lyons Bakery) keeps the responsibility himself. Often the job is given to the chief public relations executive (British Oxygen, David Brown, Tube Investments, Chase Manhattan, Koninklijke Zout Organon). One food company did this for a while, but then the marketing manager left the company and responsibility passed to six product group managers. Within a few months any semblance of consistency had disappeared. In another company, the chairman handed the follow through over to the marketing manager. All went well for several months. Then he left the company and another took his place whose views were different. The scheme changed direction at once, and now hardly resembles the original idea.

This points to the next two essentials. The board, seeing the need for continuity, must legislate for it. One step is to write down quite clearly the line to be followed. The other is to appoint the original designers for a period of time as consultants to provide and maintain the essential continuity of standards. This will also ensure that a high quality of work is sustained. The design scheme must be followed through with understanding and with due quality. If the design consultants are appointed to carry the scheme through, local arguments about who should design specific items should disappear. Individual designers can be appointed by the responsible executive, with the advice of the consultants, on the basis of quality. A good deal of design work in industry now is of poor quality, so one of the outside consultants' contributions may be to introduce a higher standard of design than has been evident in the organization before. Mediocre designers may have been used in the past who are not qualified to continue a scheme with a new-found sense of quality. Only when many of the practical applications have been completed by skilled designers, and when they have prepared definite standards for others to follow, can one turn over the continuing work to less experienced people.

It used to be thought by consultant designers that once they had produced a design manual their work was done; but this view is changing. Designers are finding that a good corporate identity scheme must be flexible. They feel the need more and more to design the various manifestations themselves – to create the variety where it is called for and, at the same time, to keep pushing the standards higher. Corporate communications are essentially dynamic. The task is never really finished. The best schemes have a strong element of continuity, but change and grow as time goes by. Henry Dreyfuss has designed for Bell Telephone for 30 years. Milner Gray has been retained by Watneys, the British brewery, for 15 years. Standards set at the start won't necessarily be right 15 or 30 years later.

Charrington United Breweries, recognizing this, formally commissioned their consultants to tour the UK to review the results of three years' work introducing the corporate identity. The designers were able to make numerous recommendations for change and improvement in the light of practical experience, having seen how local architects and others handled their design schemes in practice.

This understanding of continuity is important. Evidently it must be based on a good two-way flow of information. The company making the design acts, then watches the reaction. In a different context, this point is clarified by Dr Eric Berne in his book *The Games People Play*. He says:

> . . . communication proceeds smoothly as long as transactions are complementary. . . . [The corollary he states is:] As long as transactions are complementary communication can, in principle, proceed indefinitely.

In corporate communication work the organization concerned should recognize the need to create conditions in which these continuous and complementary 'transactions' can take place.

The design consultant carries responsibility for this, too. His design proposals should include recommendations for an internal organization to handle continuation work, and clear recommendations for future action. This means having an outline plan for handling work in a methodical way. There are obvious economies in time and money if work is put together into logical groups. This grouping may be by company or department within the organization, but in general it is much better to group work by its type. For example, building signs, including fascias, and directional and internal signing, might be handled as one exercise. Designing liveries for all vehicles

The quality of design has an obvious, though neglected, influence on impressions conveyed to people. This ad, directed by John Massey of the Container Corporation of America and donated to the City, expresses an aspect of Chicago and the services it offers citizens.

is the first letter of the alphabet
there are twenty-five more
the chicago public library has all of them
in some very interesting combinations

could constitute another group of design work. Stationery another. Standards for use of the corporate identity in advertising could make another. And so on. In each case the company can save time by predicting the need for accurate drawings and references of all material now in use. For example, to design a new livery for vehicles, one needs accurate dimension drawings of each type of vehicle in use. The transport manager probably holds these drawings. If not, they are available from the vehicle manufacturers. But they do need to be asked and waited for. All the company stationery must be gathered together. The more material which can be processed at one time the greater the degree of rationalization possible, with consequent economy.

Within any general scheme there will be particular problems. It is better to isolate them from the whole for separate consideration, than to hold up design of a mass of items while each difficulty is resolved. It is in this way, by knowing how to process a lot of design work quickly and well, that the experienced design consultant is distinguished from the less experienced. It is important to cut down the normal time taken in the design process when implementing a corporate identity design because there are often just too many items to linger over. Any big company uses hundreds (some even thousands) of different forms and pieces of paper.

In their outline plan presented when design recommendations are made, the designers should indicate the time likely to be taken by each group of work, and should arrange it in a proper sequence.

F H K Henrion and Alan Parkin, who were responsible for the redesign and coordination of a new corporate image for KLM and then advised BEA on a new identification system, have done interesting work in this field. They have broken the problem into four phases: making a survey; information storage and retrieval; formulating a brief; and planning and estimating for design development.

They say there are three basic activities to making a survey: 1. Analyse the present situation. 2. Assess it. 3. Clarify the corporate aims and their relative priorities. Analysing the present situation, they say, is:

> . . . largely a matter of listing all the design items which will or might be affected, and grouping them.

Blue Circle Cement, they cite for example, has 1800 items of stationery, 1100 vehicles, 150 packages, over 100 publications, and signs of all kinds – too many to sort out individually. Henrion and Parkin recommend putting the lot on a card system and arranging it in a way to give the basic pattern. Cards can be designed to form questionnaires which can be filled in by those with best knowledge of the items themselves.

The grouping should be design oriented, they claim, so that items in the same group should have roughly the same design needs. (In most cases this will be different from the firm's normal grouping.)

During a design programme large amounts of information need to be stored and related. They do it, broadly, by subject classification and indexing.

Using the UDC (Universal Decimal Classification), they assign each item a number according to its subject. Or they may prefer to use a system of information coordinate indexing, the 'keyword' system developed by Shell, in which information contained in each item is broken into elementary units and stored alphabetically.

To retrieve information, an enquiry is broken up into keyword units. Index cards for these keywords can be examined. Any number common to all the cards refers to an item covering that enquiry.

The design library set up for the Post Office by Henrion contains items of two main kinds; specially written cards, and all other kinds (reports, photos, and specimens). There are two kinds of cards used: blue for objects and pink for persons. They have been designed to form a questionnaire which can be sent out for completion by people responsible for the items. Non-card items are numbered in the same sequence as these, but with an X prefix.

The point of all this is to relate information that may be known separately, but which takes on a new significance in combination. But, Henrion and Parkin point out:

> Design items are controlled by people . . . it is important that co-ordination of people should precede co-ordination of items.

When they plan a programme of work and estimate its time and costs, they use a network method, breaking the work into small steps and describing each step in a numbered box. The steps are shown in sequence. They establish a minimum, maximum, and probable time for each. They distinguish between 'internal' (designer) time and 'external' (client) time, these, put together, give an 'elapsed' time for each step and the whole job. When a definite completion date is fixed by the client, they prepare a critical path.

What is the best way to arrange this sequence, or work programme? The answer depends on several factors; the most important is the timing thought best to introduce the scheme. There are two main alternatives, with variations. One attitude taken is to introduce the new corporate identity with a bang – attracting attention with a sudden impact of publicity and of change. The other approach is to let the new designs filter onto the market with or without any firm plan of introduction. How do you choose which to do? To introduce a new design scheme in one blast is to attract the most attention. Press, advertising, employee-relations effort, all focused on introducing a scheme on one day, can undoubtedly command interest. In Sweden the Co-operative movement introduced a new visual identity with tremendous impact in the space of a few weeks. Sudden change and sudden awareness of change was an important element in the scheme's effectiveness. Within twelve months 89 per cent of the Swedish population knew to whom the symbol belonged.

When Albert Heijn introduced their scheme in the Netherlands the change was reported in the newspapers. The same happened with Lyons in the UK. When a public company which had been mysteriously close about its business suddenly changed with a splash, which included girls bursting forth from a giant cake at a press conference, people were interested.

Sudden change can be expensive, but there are times when it pays off, even though it may mean wasting older material. There are occasions when the sooner one can make the change the better. There are also times when a change of design is one of the few newsworthy events that can happen to a company, and it may be decided that this news value is worth paying for. More particularly, a sudden change can be used to introduce a new product or to breathe new life into a static market situation.

Alan Elkes, the chairman of Elkes Biscuits in Uttoxeter (an English Midland town known mainly for its racecourse), linked the introduction of his new corporate identity with a special promotion of certain of his products in new packaging. Public relations effort was synchronized to this, as was trade advertising, a sales conference, and a thorough programme of employee relations. A slide presentation was prepared to explain to the staff the reasons for change. The introduction was well made, and sales increased significantly.

The Smiths Food Group also introduced their new name (it had previously been 'Smiths Potato Crisps Ltd') and new identity to coincide with their new packaging. Supported by strong TV advertising and design, the company claimed back a lost share of the market. Timing the new product introduction was determined by marketing considerations. The marketing director had to weigh the cost of synchronizing the corporate identity introduction. One cost, for example, was some £30,000 ($72,000) of wasted packaging supplies. But he judged the total impact worth it. L E Morey, at that time marketing director, explains his decision this way:

> In changing a corporate identity I believe that there are two principal considerations which favour a gradual phasing out of the old and easing in the new. One is the fear of losing existing consumer support and the other the ability to spread the cost.
>
> In our case, for tactical reasons, we decided to make our change as near as possible overnight.
>
> The problem facing the company at the time was one of image rather than product – it was emotional as opposed to rational. The change was fundamentally necessary and was therefore planned as an integral part of our promotional programme. Some months earlier the company had regained the initiative in the industry by the exploitation of new flavours and it was highly desirable to maintain this newly won momentum. Additionally the impact of the sudden change was proof positive to the employees, the trade, the consumers and the shareholders that Smiths was, in fact, a reorganised, revitalised and forward-looking company.

If there is a likely commercial advantage to a sharp, concentrated introduction then it is worth incurring some apparent loss. But industry must accept the consequences. To make such an introduction work, it should be supported in every possible way. To economize at this point is to throw away a rare opportunity.

An excellent example of a sudden and very effective change was made by Tunnel Cement. The first public intimation of change occurred on a Friday evening when all employees received a leaflet explaining the reasons for change, showing what it would look like. The next day a colourful brochure was mailed to their 4500 shareholders and about 5000 merchants, users, engineers, architects, and others. The mailing was timed to arrive on doormats and desks on Monday morning. On that Monday press stories appeared in the financial pages of newspapers. The same morning, all the company's drivers were given leaflets with illustrations of the newly designed cement sacks to hand out as they delivered the new sacks from newly painted vehicles. Part of this process had included painting vehicles in the new livery some months before, photographing them, then repainting them again, all in an attempt to preserve an element of surprise. J A D Thom, sales director of Tunnel Cement, said:

> We aimed at a big impact in one 'go' mainly because we felt effect would be lost if we introduced the new symbol gradually. We tried to time the introduction of new stationery, invoices, statements, match covers, writing pads and also signs on rail wagons to coincide. In fact, it is impossible to achieve 100 per cent change because, for example, it takes a long time to repaint a lorry fleet and still maintain adequate service. This also applies to Works signs and signs on depot silos.

Even with this degree of preparation, it is practically impossible to change everything at once. The process continues for many months, as building signs, door handles, uniforms, and all other manifestations are changed. Therefore, client and designer together must decide which items can and should be changed in time for the launch. They must bear in mind that the longer an introduction is delayed the more economical it will be, but the harder it becomes to guard secrecy or have news value.

If an introduction with impact is required, the design programme should concentrate on items which can be introduced quickly: standards for advertising, press release kits, stationery, perhaps packaging, vehicle liveries, design of central print matter, and so on. These can be introduced together and will have impact. Other items can be phased in as they are redesigned, or to fit development programmes.

At the other end of the scale is the no-fuss, gentle improvement process; as one sign is taken down another goes up; when paper runs low stocks are ordered with the new design. This is the most economical approach; it is also the slowest and least effective. Not only does it cast all the responsibility for recognizing and understanding on the viewer, it also defeats its own goal by living side by side with the old design for a long time. In a company of any size or complexity it takes time to change over totally. But one should try to speed the natural process.

To move at a measured pace like this may be necessary for reasons of cost (even though companies allocate money for change). In this event, the designers may plan to tackle the task of implementation by designing first the items that take longest to change (for example, product identification and architecture).

So one sees the priorities for action dictated by the policy of introduction, and the attitude to change.

Some companies change over slowly, and make no fuss because they fear the dangers that change might bring: 'If we change, people who buy from us now will stop buying from us.' The remedy such people see is to introduce change very gradually, in a slow series of indistinguishable alterations. Circumstances may exist when this is the right policy, but they are more rare than people think. The policy of gradual change can, in fact, be more expensive and appreciably more muddling. If customers, buyers, staff, and others are not told of changes taking place, they may be confused by them. And, almost certainly, potential benefits are dissipated.

Hesitation to push through change arises from a misconception of the relative effectiveness of the change. Executives often want to avoid abrupt shocks, so they think it wise to introduce change gently. In fact, there are at least four reasons why this fear may be unfounded. First, the time it takes to change attitudes, even about subjects with which we are most concerned. Second, the apparent lack of interest some people have in receiving a message. Third, the competitive environment in which all communications work. A most intense, concentrated effort by a company becomes diffused and weakened by the battering competition around it. Fourth, the impossibility of anything but a gradual change anyway. If a decision is taken this minute to change everything in a firm, it will still be several years before the job is complete. So practical logistics impose their own phased changeover.

Industry can move much faster than it thinks prudent. It is right to do so. Further, even with a steady development programme it should be introduced to the public at some fairly early stage and that is what usually happens. In a big or complex organization abrupt total change is difficult. Therefore, the best method is to introduce the scheme as soon as there is something to show. This introduction should be planned carefully to make the most of the opportunity it presents to make favourable contact with staff, customers, suppliers, shareholders, Press, and others. Well handled, it can herald change that is to everyone's advantage, so that people will go on looking for further signs of progress as time passes.

The designers' recommendations should include advice about the timing of an introduction, and the material that may be required for it. As well as actual corporate identity work, this should include other items to tell various audiences what is going on. The audiences to be covered include:

1. *Employees and staff.* Material may include posters for works notice boards, a letter from the chairman, a leaflet showing what is planned,

Westinghouse has one of the most far-reaching corporate design policies in the world. The new symbol (b) has eliminated unnecessary complications and now appears on everything. Designers: Paul Rand and Eliot Noyes. The old symbol for Tunnel Cement was, simply, a tunnel. To strengthen recognition of the company's products, Tunnel had introduced red stripes on packaging and elsewhere. The new symbol (d) uses these stripes in a big red 'T', in a simple form appropriate to the construction industry. The old symbol has been discarded. Designer: John Harris.

(a)

(b)

(c)

(d)

a film strip or slide presentation to show the changes envisaged. Special material may be needed for salesmen, who will be among those most concerned with meeting people outside the company.

2. *Dealers, distributors, retailers.* Trade advertising plus a letter or leaflet, and all or some of the manifestations they recognize as being the company's. Shell International, with 250,000 employees and dealers, prepared a film, filmstrip and several booklets.

3. *Consumers.* Consumer advertising is desirable, a PR campaign certainly is, with the organization and material these require.

4. *Shareholders, the city.* Advertising in business publications or in the financial section of newspapers; brochure, letter from the chairman, PR.

5. *Creative agencies and those responsible for implementing the schemes.* They need a clear explanation of the company's intention to implement the scheme effectively. This means that at least preliminary design standards must be prepared for them.

6. *Suppliers*, often forgotten, can be proud spokesmen for a company if they feel involved in its growth. Efforts should be made to explain to them what the company is doing and what effect this may have on their relations.

Numerous other audiences (universities, schools, government bodies, trade associations) should be informed. Much of this work can be undertaken in the course of normal planned PR activity.

The consultant designers can tell clients of their experience in this field, but ideally the introduction should be conducted by professional public and industrial relation officers, furnished with material by the designers. They must keep clearly in mind the basic communication goal agreed by the company. As a first step in the drive for continuity, the executive responsible for corporate identity should be involved in any introduction.

We have seen that when designers present their proposed design solution, clients should know what happens next. The recommendations, we've noted, should include an internal organization, a draft work plan to implement the scheme, and suggestions for the timing of an introduction.

The company will need to consider the cost of other applications, but the designers have, at least, provided it with information on which to base decisions. It happens too often that resistance to the scheme builds up somewhere in the organization: there are always good reasons for not doing something, particularly when one's own autonomy is threatened. Bearing in mind the conservatism of most people, and their ignorance of the power of good communications, it is understandable that opposition should arise. Sometimes the criticism or caution is justified, in which case the designers should recognize as much. The situation is not unusual, and it is as well to realize the fact. The answer must lie as we have said before, in the firmness of the chairman or chief executive officer.

Some corporate identity projects are embarked on either when companies merge, or when a group of companies, loosely controlled, is to be drawn more tightly together. In these cases, the desire for unity is not shared by everyone, neither is the willingness to sacrifice control. The image of unity is false – the sign of unity an aspiration rather than a fact.

The answer to this is not to progress at the pace of the slowest, most obdurate member of the group, like a half-speed and vulnerable wartime ship convoy. In any organization, only a few people have forward vision, and still fewer see the strength of unified communications. Looking forward, trying to shift the organization to a posture it will need to have at some point in the future, often means that there will be a gap between present reality and the recommended corporate identity goals.

Corporate identity schemes cannot be handled in a fully delegated, democratic way. Someone must rule what is to be done, and the work must be strictly controlled from one central position. The corporate identity then becomes a vehicle for establishing the unity that is required. Not all companies in a group need have a unified look: they may be quite diverse and unrelated. But even that must be a policy decision by the chief executive. If the need for tactics remains, the right thing to do is to isolate the unbending – give them a measured amount of time to fall in with the progress made in other areas.

It is necessary to restate the need for strong executive control in a chapter devoted to implementation because the primary reason for poor implementation is poor executive control. Too often the designer finds himself trying to steer through a consistent design policy in the face of opposition and without the clear executive backing that would make his work easier.

It is at this implementation stage that support is imperative because the designers are daily meeting department heads, their assistants, suppliers, and others, all with their own opinions of what ought to be done. Satisfying them all is impossible. It is not always even desirable, and it is extremely time consuming.

A requirement, therefore, of effective implementation is a statement by the chairman stating unequivocally what he wants done. A further important aid is the establishment of a manual which lays down all the design standards required. The next chapter discusses such manuals, and describes a few successful ones.

11

An analysis of corporate identity manuals

There are a number of reasons for disseminating the fact of a new corporate identity scheme. Above all others is the need to establish the scheme within the organization involved, to tell people who must use the new design what it means and how to handle it. Unless the total design programme is properly carried through it won't even survive, much less work. One states the obvious because even today some companies think that, given the concept, they have enough. Admittedly, they save the cost of a design manual, which pleases them, but experience shows that they risk losing everything else.

The corporate identity manual is essential to any company or organization seriously concerned with projecting itself in a planned, consistent way. It can vary in complexity from case to case, but it cannot be dispensed with. Even the smallest companies, trade associations, or groups should write down their communication goals, showing how they intend to use design to help achieve them, and to provide specific guidance for printers and others.

The corporate identity manuals reviewed here are all from large organizations: the Swedish Co-operative movement, a retailing group with the problem of getting hundreds of near-autonomous societies throughout the country to express themselves consistently; UniRoyal, a manufacturer concerned with changing an unsatisfactory name internationally; Eastern Airlines, a modern service organization who want to see that their new policy is followed through effectively; and British Rail, a nationalized industry anxious to change, but with very large numbers and varieties of manifestation, and huge investments in capital equipment. In preparing this section a number of other manuals have been studied, at least three of which have been rendered obsolete by mergers. The saddest is that of AEI, the large British engineering group: the manual was redundant the day it was published (as its author was a few weeks later) when the group merged with GEC. This highlights the need to keep an open-minded and flexible policy of identification.

It is harder than ever before for companies to know where they may find themselves, what fields they may be in, who they may join. At least three corporate identity manuals in course of preparation at the time of writing, to the author's knowledge, are based on that outlook. Each shows how variations, as yet unrequired and unimagined, including corporate names, could be incorporated into the essential scheme without damage to it.

Design action need not be delayed because a merger may make it obsolete. The designers should simply recognize the possibility and design accordingly. While this is given new point by today's rash of mergers, diversifications, and expansions, it has always been true, and all these changes should be expressed visually. On this subject F H K Henrion wrote:

> Almost all designers complain that their original conceptions end up misunderstood, misapplied and watered down; and this is because an agreed scheme soon ceases to meet requirements and is altered without reference to the designer.

There is a continuing need for adjustment and improvement even when basic principles have been established.

At no time should a corporate identity programme be considered finished. Manuals should not be looked on as static statements, like the smile frozen for 300 years on the Mona Lisa. They should be seen as the most up-to-date answer to a continually changing question. At the same time a strong continuity and consistency is required. The economics of change, particularly where capital equipment is involved, make continuity necessary. For another thing, we can only hope to register an identity and have it understood if it is sustained for years. Mary Quant, whose pre-eminence depends on leading fashions which change every few months, has sustained a consistent visual identity for six years and expects to keep the same for some years more.

The corporate manual is the best way to ensure that standards are established and *maintained*. It must be designed for use by the people who will implement the scheme. Not all of them will be Harvard graduates. Young studio artists, vehicle sign-writers, and suppliers of all kinds will be among people using the book, so it must be easy to understand. Protagonists see these manuals in different ways. Some books have a strong element of persuasion about them. Some are vastly complex, others too simple to be useful.

Because cases vary so much it is risky to list too many rules. A good corporate manual must contain a clear statement from a senior executive saying what is being done and why, and urging the cooperation of everyone concerned to implement the scheme. It should have a clear index system: each page should be numbered and easy to refer to. It should be bound in a loose-leaf or ring binder, so that new sheets can be inserted and old ones removed. It should state specifically the items that are mandatory and must be adhered to. It should state any areas that may be left to discretion and those which must be approved by a central authority. It should state who is responsible for maintaining standards in the organization and to whom questions must be addressed.

A corporate identity manual should show the company's symbol, if there is one, in black and white and in reverse, preferably with a grid to show how to draw and enlarge it. The logotype, if there is one, should be shown similarly. Letterstyles for the company, divisions, and departments, as appropriate, should be shown, with precise details of spacing, and weights. Colours should be shown exactly. The relationships of the various items must be specified accurately. Some manuals show them, but lay down no dimensions or rules to guide the user, leaving too much to chance, permitting more tolerance than is desirable.

The manual will then show the design scheme applied to various manifestations. They must be specific, detailed, and precise. Exact dimensions and relationships must be shown. The purpose of the manual is to show people how to carry out the design scheme so that the organization can express itself the same way everywhere. The more that is left to the reader to decide the more variations will arise. Some manuals, particularly American ones, show the dos and don'ts. If the manual is clearly written this is unnecessary, but it does stress the need to follow the manual to the letter. Most good manuals not only state the source of supply of references, but provide sheets of them, perforated to be torn out as required.

It is impossible to legislate for good design; even within one company the goals can vary to suit various audiences. When women buy dresses, underwear, stockings, shoes, berets, and cosmetics bearing the Mary Quant label they are buying from a young, very individual designer. But when her company becomes a public one, the communication problem will alter. Shareholders may look for a strong management team: doubtless the company will stress its organizational and financial strength (in 1966 Mary Quant's retail sales exceeded £5 million). According to Alexander Plunket Greene, who shares executive responsibility with chairman Archie McNair, 'We're gently leaning over to presenting ourselves as an organization.' Mary Quant's OBE brought 'more personal publicity than I'd like,' he admitted, even though he finds the swinging London thing still helps. It is clear that one company may have different and indeed diametrically opposed communication goals to suit its needs. As far as possible the design manual should cater for this, and provide practical guidance.

The contents of the General Mills corporate identity manual is typical. In a loose-leaf binder, it incorporates: *Section one.* Corporate Mark, A Statement from the President, Purpose of the Manual, Usage of the Mark – Authorized color, Reverse, Backgrounds, Size: Ratio, Maximum, Minimum, Reproduction Art, Containing Shapes, Color Standards, Grid Scale. *Section two*. Use of Signature in Advertising and Promotion, General Notes, Use with Divisional Signatures, TV Applications. *Section three*. Use of Signature in Packaging, Consumer, Institutional, Industrial. *Section four*. Booklets and Brochures. *Section five*. Stationery and Forms. *Section six*. Signage. *Section seven*. Transportation. *Section eight*. International.

The purpose of the manual is made quite clear. The foreword says:

> This manual has been prepared as a guide for all who are charged with the implementation and maintenance of the company's corporate identification. Established herein are regulations devised to insure a uniform application of the new symbol for maximum impact, a strong family look and at the same time to provide sufficient versatility so that creativeness in usage is not thwarted.
>
> The program for the proper application and use of the new symbol will go into effect immediately. It is essential that the regulations be given careful study and consideration by those individuals, within General Mills, its divisions, subsidiaries, advertising and design departments . . . as well as outside advertising agencies, public relations counsel and other suppliers . . . who are responsible for the use of graphics.
>
> Any questions arising out of situations not covered in this manual should be addressed to. . . .

Notwithstanding the quaint language, the essentials are there: *who* the manual is for, *what* it is to do, *why* it has been created, *when* it goes into use, and *where* to go for help.

MacMillan Bloedal, a large Canadian timber firm, incorporates three other helpful ideas in its manual. There is a glossary of terms, so that the words used in the manual are understood the same way by everyone; there is a description of the symbol which says why it has been designed as it has: and throughout the most precise text, specifying in some instances, to $\frac{1}{32}$ inch, runs an explanation of why the manifestation described is important to the company's image. The introduction to this manual is signed by the chairman and chief executive officer who puts the full weight of his office behind the manual. He uses the same imperatives we saw from General Mills:

> . . . your cooperation in adhering to the forms shown is essential if it is to identify accurately the company and its products in the public mind.

Moreover, he adds a full and interesting description of why he wants the job done.

The Swedish Co-operative movement, claimed to be the largest business enterprise in Sweden (300 consumer Co-operative Societies, 27 per cent of all retail food sales in Sweden), took $2\frac{1}{2}$ years to develop a new corporate identity. They claim it is no less than 'a new and vital factor in marketing'. Their design manual is a 32-page booklet printed in two and sometimes three colours on glossy paper. It cannot be added to and shows principles and examples more than precise details. Instead, it states where references for each item may be obtained. The introduction states the need for a unified identity:

> Consumer co-operation is Sweden's largest concern – in itself proof of the soundness of the co-operative idea.
>
> But much is needed to hold the picture together. There is a danger that the individual consumer does not see where our movement starts and ends. Diffuse limits reduce our competitive strength.
>
> We must create a sharply defined image for the concern, and a common symbol can contribute towards giving the public a clearer picture of the total resources of consumer co-operation.
>
> An image programme of these dimensions stretches over several years. However, the aim is, with correct planning, to make an effective introduction starting in 1967.
>
> This, then, is largely an *economically* necessary measure to increase our competitive strength. The standards described here show that great efforts have been made to find an effective and attractive design.
>
> The Administrative Council, Board and Marketing Council hope that this image programme will receive 100 per cent support and a flying start. We all know that today's customers and consumers seek advice and purchasing security. Our new symbol will show them the way.

The next page describes the 'infinity' symbol and states: '[It] may only be used on the condition that the following rules are carefully followed. . . .' Later pages show examples of correct and wrong use of the symbol. The problem is complicated because the structure of the Co-operative movement involves many societies, with different names. They have felt the need to distinguish between 'concerns' which use the symbol with the name, and brand names, which do not.

Throughout the text is firm. For example:

> . . . the Consumer cooperative symbol may not be altered in form or colour or in some other way presented in a manner which deviates from the determined appearance. . . .

The symbol is drawn on graph paper to show its exact proportions. Two blues have been chosen, one for exterior and another for interior use. Both are specified exactly. Readers are advised how to employ the colours, but the rules laid down are general. They make it clear that the house colour is to be used mainly for permanent purposes, that temporary sales measures can be in other colours, and that: 'in all respects the merchandise must dominate and must never be overshadowed by the blue colour . . .'.

Typography shown in the Co-operative manual is for use on outdoor signs, direction signs, and permanent in-store texts. Principles for its use are described and an alphabet is enclosed in a pocket in the back cover of the book. Principles, too, are laid down for the use of the symbol and lettering externally, though perhaps more reliance is placed on the discretion of local societies than is ideal. For example:

When used in architectural connections the symbol and typeface shall have the aim of achieving the greatest possible graphic effect.

Although further details follow, this statement is open to wide variety of interpretation.

It is interesting that the use of other materials is covered. Aluminium and stainless steel are preferred. Gold metals, the manual says, 'have not such a good symbolic connection with the image . . . and should be avoided'.

Flags, vehicle identification, packaging, stationery, receipts envelopes, cash receipts, and even prepaid postage franking stamps are included in the manual. It appears that there are no rules for applying the 'infinity' symbol to the packaging, except that it should be there, and less important than the brand name and product information. The manual states changeover periods and target dates for completion of the main applications.

The Swedish Co-operative scheme was developed under the direction of the marketing council, by a small group including the advertising agency's creative director, the head of the Co-op's design office, the exhibition designer, and a general secretary.

As a result of careful planning, the whole identification was launched in Sweden during 1967 with tremendous force. Posters were used, as were a hundred or more advertisements in newspapers, point-of-sale material, and cinema advertising. How successful has it been? During the first year of its introduction, five national opinion polls were conducted in Sweden. Two weeks after the first appearance of the new symbol (mid January 1967) 42 per cent recognized it. The figure rose to 57 per cent in February, 71 per cent in April, 82 per cent in September, and by December to 89 per cent.

They were anxious to identify a consumer benefit with the new symbol – a purchase guarantee. Goods bought in any Co-operative shop in Sweden could be returned or exchanged in any other. By December 54 per cent of the people interviewed associated this customer guarantee with the new symbol. A remarkable accomplishment, and it was recognized as such. Count Sigvard Bernadotte remarked: 'I have never seen the introduction of a new symbol carried out in a more thorough and rational manner.'

How much did it all cost? The Co-operative calculate the first phase (research, planning, and preparation) cost £40,000 ($96,000). The second phase (permanent new signs for all Co-operative shops and Domus department stores, and repainting vehicles), cost nearly £400,000 ($960,000). Introducing the symbol cost about £300,000 ($720,000).

Across the world, US Rubber had the courage to undertake the vast task of changing its name completely. More, it decided to replace a number of often well-established local identities with one global identity.

The corporate identity manual published to help accomplish this is a model for the practical and simple guidance it provides. About 100 sheets printed on light board and grouped in 14 sections, are contained in an extremely rugged ring binder. It will last and can be added to. It starts with a simple explanation of corporate identity, explaining why the company has chosen its new name.

UniRoyal is the foundation upon which we are building a new corporate identity for our company. Four years of research have proved that UniRoyal is a name which is highly suitable for us. It is easily spoken. It is visually pleasing. It connotes diversity without product restrictions. It has no geographical limitations. . . .

The introduction explains the need for consistent use of one identity, and charges that accomplishing this 'is the responsibility of each member of the worldwide UniRoyal family . . .'.

The next page describes the purpose and use of the manual and names the central authority – the 'Office of Corporate Identity' in New York, giving the address and telephone number to which all questions should be directed. It then gives definitions of the main words: corporate trademark, corporate name, and brand trademarks.

The next section describes the corporate trademark, both in words and by illustration. Again, a firm statement:

The placement of the lettering within the rectangle as well as the proportions of the rectangle are carefully designed for maximum legibility and visual balance. *They should not be altered in any way.* [Author's italics.]

The next page states a minimum size: 'The symbol must not be reproduced in a size smaller than $\frac{3}{4}''$ in width.' A drawing makes this point still plainer. It then states how the colours should be used, ruling that any exceptions should be cleared by the office of corporate identity. The next pages discuss background colours and specify the minimum space that must surround the trademark, which is described as 'the area of isolation'. Incorrect uses of the trademark are shown and described and the correct symbol is shown on a grid.

Because of the change, usage of the new corporate name, both in the US and in other countries, is described carefully.

The manual states when to use the *trademark*: advertisements, catalogues, products, and labels, literature, signs on plants and offices, packaging, internal bulletins, external bulletins, trucks and other vehicles, souvenirs, calling cards, stationery (with corporate name), news release headings, publication mastheads. The *corporate name*, it says, should be used on legal contracts and documents. Stationery (with trademark), telephone listings, first paragraph of news release, company cheques, business forms. These lists, although incomplete, are a concrete help to bewildered executives about the world.

Division names are spelled out.

124

The next section describes the design of stationery and forms, and shows how to lay out the typing on a letter.

Each month UniRoyal ship 600,000 cases of branded products from its plants around the world. The company attaches importance to identifying them correctly. In fact, the company has set up an 'Identity and Packaging Committee', to coordinate all packaging design. A section in the manual lays down guidelines for general use. It lays down no rigid specifications for labelling, because labels themselves vary so much. However, all labels for company-endorsed products carry the corporate trademark and conform to the graphic principles outlined in the manual. They are approved by the office of corporate identity before use.

The manual says:

Wherever possible a family resemblance should be developed not only through the use of corporate trademark but throughout coordinating colour design.

Although ten illustrations follow, this section is a little too vague to achieve either the consistency which UniRoyal seeks, or the quality they'd like.

The next section covers use of the new name in advertising. The trademark is to appear in every advertisement, in the bottom righthand corner. Variations to this are allowed only if approved by the director of advertising. Readers are warned of incorrect use of the trademark: too light, too small, against too dark a background, in the wrong colours, too close to other marks.

There is a page on the use of the corporate trademark in TV advertising (in 10–39-second spots with audio identification. In 1-minute spots both video and audio identification although not necessarily synchronized.) All uses of the name in TV advertising are cleared both by the director of advertising and the director of corporate identity.

Other sections cover sales promotion material, signs and vehicles, displays and exhibitions. In each case principles are shown, but details are not defined enough to ensure that all manifestations are well done; it would be possible to follow the manual to the letter but still produce bad designs. This is a weakness in UniRoyal's corporate identity scheme which they may wish to overcome in other ways as time goes by.

There is no reason why a whole scheme should be held up until every detail is sorted out. You have to start somewhere. The essence of the design manual is that it lays down the rules where those exist. It may add to them later, as the designers have time to go into new areas of the company. But if any organization wants a good, consistent visual identity it cannot be content with vague or incomplete statements, except as a temporary expedient.

UniRoyal has chosen a colour-matching system available, they say, from printers in eighty-five cities, and has supplied purchasing officers with addresses of these firms. The manual gives the printing ink formulas for both coated and uncoated papers and provides several perforated sheets of colour swatches to match. This is necessary because the same inks can appear quite different – as different as Oxford and Cambridge blues – on different surfaces.

Another section in this manual states ways of using brand names. It points out:

> The company's trademarks and brand names are among its most valuable properties. Misuse of these marks can result in their loss as was the case with such marks as Aspirin, Lanolin and Cellophane.

It distinguishes between the company's own trademark and product trademarks. Ideally, it says, one supports the other. A widely known product can help sell products which are less known and have little advertising support. The manual advises on the choice of trademarks, and lays down a procedure to be followed before they are used (obtaining legal clearance from company lawyers and final clearance from the office of corporate identity).

A final selection in the UniRoyal manual lists materials available to all plants and branches worldwide from the office of corporate identity. These include: decals in sixteen sizes or variations, posters, embroidered emblems (in two sizes) for use on drivers jackets, uniforms, and by employees in games and athletic teams; binders for address books, telephone directories, catalogues, and management guides; and finally repro proofs of the worldwide trademark, US trademark, corporate signature, division names, worldwide signatures (UniRoyal Ltd, UniRoyal Englebert SA, UniRoyal Englebert AG, and others).

This list is enough to show the degree of penetration the corporate identity is expected to achieve. One small example, it states that all private cars bought or leased for company personnel should be white:

> No other colour should be purchased without clearance through the corporate car fleet coordinator in the purchasing department.

And all cars are to be identified: manufacturing and service with a decal on each front door; sales cars with a decal on the right rear bumper.

For all its comprehensiveness, UniRoyal's design manual is essentially a simple workbook. Eastern Airlines manual is more advanced. For one thing, it states a communication goal which is a *'unified verbal and visual expression'* of the corporation. The concept they want to communicate is: 'Substance, competence, inventive considerateness.' In a rather long preamble they describe how they may live up to these words. The preamble then goes on with the imperatives which we've seen are common to all schemes:

> *Exact* duplication of the corporation graphic elements . . . and their use as set forth in the manual is necessary.

It says professional design counsel should be sought for items not covered by the manual, and it notes areas where individual judgement may be used.

Finally, the preamble asks for questions to be channelled to the Director – Visual Communication.

Eastern's corporate identification manual is, again, contained in a ring binder, and has seventy-two pages printed on glossy paper in two or three colours. It is divided into four main sections: 1. Introduction. 2. Basic graphic standards. 3. Applications. 4. Supplementary data and correspondence.

Section 2, basic graphic standards, is itself subdivided into six parts: (a) Description of basic elements. (b) The corporate signature. (c) Colour policy. (d) Background and display control. (e) Reproduction standards. (f) Supporting material.

The basic mark is shown in its correct colour ('Ionosphere' blue) and described, with the stern note that it 'should not be used for punctuation or for frivolous decorative purposes'. The logotype is described and shown in colour. The corporate signature (symbol and logotype together) is shown, with the statement that it is 'not to be altered or changed in any way'. Alternate signatures for vertical flush left and flush right use are specified precisely. Exact letterspacing of the logotype is shown with exact dimensions to suit various type sizes. The colour policy is described, with examples of what is acceptable and what is not.

A page describes display and layout with comments many could copy to advantage:

> In keeping with good graphic design and layout practice care should always be taken to display the corporate signature in generous open space, free from interference by, or close association with any visually distracting graphic elements. No elements are to impinge upon any signature nor should a signature appear on printed textures, over-all patterns or otherwise visually conflicting backgrounds.
>
> A signature must not span two adjacent colour areas. A signature should never be enclosed in a shape. When a signature is used in reverse the colour area must be sufficient so as not to appear as an enclosing shape. A signature should not be used in punctuation, as part of a statement, or as a key element in slogans. . . .

Again the section on reproduction control is packed with sensible guidance:

> Reproduction should be made only from the original design, or from an authorised copy of the original design . . . available from the director of visual communications.
>
> It is desirable that the mark and signature should always be reproduced in solid colour. However, conditions exist (such as newspaper advertising) when screen tone reproduction is required. In such cases a signature should never be less than 80 per cent black. The minimum permissible screen size for satisfactory legibility varies with the coarseness of screen. As a general rule, a coarse screen should not be applied to any signature whose logotype is less than $1\frac{7}{8}$ inches long. . . .

The manual contains sheets of the signature in various sizes and arranged in different ways suitable for reproduction. For large-scale reproduction the signature, in a number of forms, is shown on numbered grids.

The manual is emphatic that the letterform of the logotype is not to be used for any other purpose. Supporting statements, it says, should be set in Univers 65 (Monotype Univers bold 693). Alternative faces it suggests are Standard medium or Helvetica medium. Suggested treatment of stronger and less strong statements is given. For special promotion purposes other typefaces may be used for their special characteristics.

The section on applications shows simple sketches of markings on all types of aircraft in Eastern's fleet, ground equipment, a curiously old-fashioned and Russian-looking collection of 'wings' for air and ground crew, and very detailed instructions on the correct identification of city ticket offices. These show 'primary' and 'secondary' exteriors and interiors, specified to the extent of showing the height from the ground and frequency of individual 'frosted glass' marks. Airport ticket offices are also specified. Identification of executive offices is covered, including the use of materials, down to the size and positioning of individual room numbers. Alarmingly, the layout of a typical VIP room is shown. There are thirty-five items in it (including plant, TV bench, TV set, bar storage, coffee table, sofa, lounge chairs, and wastepaper basket just to the left of the desk).

Stationery is shown cursorily though perhaps sufficiently.

British Rail's manual, the last we'll look at, is far more detailed in this and every respect. Created by Design Research Unit, under the direction of Milner Gray, it leaves little room for misuse of the railway's main visual elements. Running into three volumes, each in a ring binder, it specifies precise details for almost every conceivable application. What colour to paint the inside of cowl ventilators on ships? It's stated. When to take down flags and how to store and clean them? It's detailed.

British Rail's design manual starts with a statement by the chairman which explains why change is necessary and asks for support for it:

> The future of British Railways depends upon what the travelling public and industry think of them, to create the right public impression we have to provide good service and also present an appearance of smartness and efficiency. Neither is a substitute for the other – both are necessary.
>
> The best way of creating the right visual impression for all organisations as widespread as ours is the consistent use of the same well designed distinguishing features wherever they can appropriately be embodied. This gives cumulative impact to the features used, causes the organisation's facilities to be easily recognised, and produces a corporate identity which reflects the unity of the organisation behind all our activities. . . .
>
> The way in which all the features should be applied, to achieve consistency of effect over our whole system, is set out in this manual and I am sure that I can rely upon all concerned to see that our corporate identity

One of the best-known symbols in the world. Simple, timeless.

programme is carried out with sustained enthusiasm and by correct use of this manual.

The British Rail second manual is divided into twelve sections: basic elements; printed publicity; architecture and signposting; rolling stock; equipment; road vehicles; ships; liner trains; uniforms; stationery; miscellaneous; and appendices including index.

The introduction recognizes that, in such a large organization, not everything can be changed quickly. It says:

> The new corporate identity is being applied initially in certain fields and predetermined priorities. By following these priorities vigorously, widespread dissemination of the basic elements will be achieved quickly.

The introduction continues by describing the new symbol, the new name (British Rail), the new lettering and the new colours. It states where to get authorization and further guidance. The section on 'Authorized Applications' lists fields, describes items, states which elements of the design to use, and when to introduce them. For example, on all publicity, exhibition, and display material, printed matter and announcements for the use of the public, staff information, working documents, etc., all items of the visual identity are to be used as appropriate. The new designs are to be introduced 'forthwith'. But the new design will be applied to ships as they are repainted, to liner trains as they are installed, to passenger rolling stock as directed and agreed by the corporate identity steering committee.

Basic elements shown in the manual are: (a) new symbol; (b) logotype; (c) alphabet; (d) house colours, authority for applications, use of symbol (how, where), use of symbol and logotype together, use of lettering, use of house colours. Subsequent pages show the symbol in black and white and in reverse, in a box, with a grid, in colour, with the logotype, and as a stencil. It is also shown on a flag, including the size of the flag, its height from ground and instructions like this:

> Flags should not be dry cleaned, nor should they be left raised overnight, but taken down at dusk, dried and rolled (not folded), and stored.

There is a special symbol for the accident-prevention service, and detailed instructions for using the symbol and logotype on posters – specifying size for each poster size and where. Several pages cover the use of the symbol and logotype with other identifications (British Rail – International Inc; Car Ferry, Hook of Holland, Motorail, Inter City, Seaspeed). Printed publicity and symbols for letterheads are shown. Credit titles for films are detailed. The name signs outside stations, illuminated signs (including method of wiring, material, light source, where to get planning permission) are described. Standard dimensions for lettering and signs are given. Station signposting is detailed exactly. Principles for the use of arrows are shown. Also specified are wall bracket signs, fascia lettering, and the method of assembly for multiworded signs.

There is a section on rolling stock with superb four-colour drawings plus colour references, and one of lineside equipment, road vehicles, and ships (British Rail has 100 ships of various kinds). The manual states the colours to paint hulls, funnels, interiors of cowl ventilators (flame red), bridge superstructures, deck-houses, overhead davits and lifecraft platforms (white). Masts, derrick posts, hatches, etc., are grey. Bollards, etc., are black.

In this most detailed manual are four-colour drawings of the markings to go on liner trains with an exact numbering system for freightliner containers. There is a section on uniforms and specific layouts for stationery. These show how to place typing on the page, when to underline and when not to.

Applications of the new identity to linen are shown, even for such quaint items as antimacassars which, the reader is told, are to be Jacquard loom in white mercurized cotton.

And still the work goes on. New pages are being added. To keep the manuals accurate and effective pages are being replaced. Incidentally British Rail hope to change the livery of their vast rolling stock in three years. And they're now using two colours instead of ten.

The British Rail manual and others we have looked at sound complicated. However, the organizations concerned have all been largely successful in implementing a new corporate identity. Unquestionably, full but clear manuals have aided them. One can say with assurance that proper design manuals which, in addition to specifying every detail, pinpoint a central position of responsibility, are indispensable. But, as Stuart Rose, who is among the designers behind the British Rail manual, has said:

A manual is not the end. The railways – or any company – is a living organism. New problems will always come up.

12

Is this only for big companies?

This book and this subject are not for big companies only. The cases quoted are mostly of large, international organizations. It may be thought that much of the research and method can only be afforded by the larger companies. Smaller companies, one might say, don't need all these complicated systems.

Smaller companies may enjoy shorter lines of communication; be closer to employees, customers, and dealers. Certainly visual communications, or efforts in any promotion media, come second to personal face-to-face contact. The smaller company has more intimate contact with its audiences, and so seems to have less need for planned corporate identity activities. It may also find itself in a niche that is not particularly interesting to larger groups. So in some ways, the smaller firm may be better off. But not in all ways.

What does 'small' mean? Bernard Wetherill MP writing in *The Times* about the need for a Small Business Development Bureau, cited companies with up to 2000 employees – a figure which to thousands of firms seems huge.

An automotive manufacturer may be too small with 50,000 employees: a management consultant or a clothing firm may be unwieldy and large with a hundredth of that number. In the absence of absolutes, size is relative. Whether an organization sees itself as large or small depends partly on the vision of its directors and staff, partly on the competition, partly on tradition (though this is evaporating as we quickly adjust to new scales of size in all areas), though mainly on its problems and the area of its operations.

The Council of Industrial Design may be cited. With about 240 staff, devoted almost exclusively to promoting design in Britain, it may be thought large. In terms of an audience of 300,000 firms and 50 million consumers, it may be considered small. Its 240 staff are almost all highly trained people, doing responsible work. To have this high proportion of skilled staff makes them large in relation to many organizations that manage with two or three. So it is easy to confuse accepted ideas of large and small. Many large companies actually have very simple communications problems. Some small firms, who see themselves as too insignificant to dwell on these matters, have complex problems which, whether they see them or not, can be important to their well-being.

It is difficult to specify general situations, but there are several developments occurring which deserve consideration.

We have dwelt on some of the larger international companies for two reasons. First, they provide lessons for everyone. Second, growing internationalism throws almost all attitudes of large and small into the waste-paper basket. Many companies, long established, secure, and famous at home, are establishing themselves in other countries where they may be none of these things. They may need to approach their communication problems with a new humility.

A famous American food firm, marketing and manufacturing internationally, is known throughout the Western world. Their policy for forty years or more, has been to establish one identity everywhere. Recently, they acquired a company in South America in a country where they were unknown. The brand name of their acquisition was better known and had $1 million (£400,000) spent on promoting it in the last four years. What should the parent do? Should it say: 'We're big everywhere, our name must replace the existing one.' Or should it admit that it will take a while to register its own name in a new market? Should it use the local one that is known, and attach its own gradually?

This is one example of how new markets can create new situations. Plenty of evidence suggests that almost all firms with international aspirations need to think afresh.

There is a real twist the other way. International firms are invading the territory of all but the smallest local manufacturers. To the smaller firm the cry is: 'Arm yourself: foreign foxes are after your chickens.' The consequence of this invasion is twofold. First, local firms must try to understand how big companies position themselves in image terms. Second, smaller firms must shape their own activities and their communications to make the most of the virtues they possess. (There are enviable advantages to being *local*, in touch with the market, and flexible, able to respond quickly to any situation.) A study into certain aspects of German banking conducted in 1962 found this. With a fraction of the financial strength, few of the services, unable to provide national coverage, one of the small private Hanoverian banks was still preferred by customers to the large, eminently respectable, Big Three banks.

It had a friendliness and concern which people felt the big ones lacked.

In London, Glyn Mills, a relatively small bank (now part of a larger group but maintaining its own identity) might be expected to provide more individual attention than the giant banks.

Here is an interesting position. A small bank is successful in so far as it is thought to have the intimacy of smallness. What would happen if they were to set out to look larger, if they aped their bigger competitors? There is a possibility that their advantage would be lost, their appeal dissipated. It is only by comprehending the communication activity of giant as well as comparable competitors that one can make the most of what opportunities there are for smaller firms.

In certain ways, smaller firms are in direct competition with the giants. Labour, for example. Why work for an uncertain local firm when you can work for one of the famous international companies that have recently settled in the community? There may be good reason. If there is, it should be made clear.

The larger firms need skilled workers and top-calibre executives. They have the resources to hire them, the personnel relations policies, the sickness, holiday, and pension benefits, the broad scale of activity, to attract and keep good people.

Unless smaller firms match these benefits with others (which may be quite different and peculiar to them: a greater sense of participation, the personal touch, less regulated conditions, the chance to help build something), they could find the gap between themselves and the giants yawning still wider. One has only to think of the 6000 US companies that have established plants abroad since 1958, half of them in Europe, to see the imminent problem. Caused by internationalism, it is a situation that business in Belgium has had to face already, and doubtless other countries have, too.

The need to attract staff is great: 301,000 people emigrated from Britain in 1967, so there is scant evidence that industry or government has much idea how to do it.

It is often thought that, no matter how worthy, smaller firms cannot afford the sophistication of a good corporate identity. In all but a handful of cases, this is untrue. It is a question of recognizing values. Many firms pay more for their managing director's car than they do on design or public relations in a year. Certainly, some companies have a greater need than others. There is an optimum level of activity, though it can hardly ever be to do *nothing*. That is to be incommunicado. Certainly, some companies don't need or cannot afford the subtle research undertaken by others. But there are many levels of valid activity between IBM and some head-in-the-sand manufacturers.

Let's cast the economic argument where it belongs. There is a huge international company, headquartered in London and with immense installations in the US, Canada, Africa, Europe, and Australia. Last year their UK profits only were £30 million. They have no corporate identity policy at all,

One of the best symbols and best exploited is the Woolmark, designed by Italy's Francesco Saroglia. Pictures show Sir Francis Chichester sporting it, and a million-tube advertisement in Paris.

employ only the smallest, least expensive design units for the print design that must be done. The reason for doing so little is, they say, cost. In a sense, this can be taken as a comfort and a spur by smaller companies that would like to act but feel unable to afford it.

This was worth mentioning for two contradictory reasons. First, attitudes to small companies are mixed. On one hand, they tend to be credited with being more personal, more likely to care about individual customers. They are credited with being quicker to respond to situations and often with being more concerned with quality – a belief deriving from the respect for craftsmen. On top of this, they have the negative virtue of not being large in an age when large companies are sometimes thought too powerful for the public good.

On the other hand, it is often felt that the smaller firm is less efficient, less advanced, less generous, less knowledgeable than larger competitors. The term 'small business' itself sounds derogatory, just as, in our prepackaged world, 'small' is less good than 'big' in many fields. But in Britain alone it includes 90 per cent of all manufacturing establishments. (According to the 1958 Census, firms employing under 500 people did 46 per cent, by value, of all industrial sales in the UK.) It also includes many of the most sophisticated service organizations in existence. Increasingly, the large organizations turn to the smaller ones for specialist advice in sophisticated areas and notably for the essential innovation it must have. According to Jewkes, Sawers, and Stillman,[1] academic studies have demonstrated that a very high proportion of inventions, even in highly sophisticated fields, have come from small concerns. An American survey, found that 50 per cent of the new inventions and processes this century have been produced by small businesses or by individuals.

This is evidence of the real value and dynamism of some, if not all, small business. For them to be thought less of for being small is plainly unjust. But it may happen by default. From the syndrome of attitudes to smaller firms, including both helpful and damaging ideas, it is clearly necessary for individual companies to extract and exploit the most appropriate.

This means using the techniques of verbal and visual communications as effectively as the best larger companies.

The policy of a Belgian advertising agency and an English design firm may reveal another danger. The agency once said it wanted to be known as a 'sort of creative bank'. The designers wanted to be known as 'the IBM of the design world'. Both statements arise naturally from the feeling that smaller firms are seen as less reliable than larger ones. In both cases, the effect of their policies could be to discourage creative people from joining them and disappoint staff they successfully recruit who, accepting them at their word, want the benefits of big firms. They may also discourage client companies who seek creative services. Thus, a predilection for size, as a virtue in itself, may lead companies into wrong decisions, and may cause their communications to be damaging to their own interests.

Confounding any attempt to find steady answers, one can also say that the opposite is true: some client companies seek the security of size. Thus, the smaller company or service organization must try to position itself in terms most truthful and most appropriate to the wishes of the potential market.

When should a company see itself and be identified with the positive aspects of largeness? When should it identify itself with the positive aspects of smallness? To say that the facts should dictate the answer is too simple. As we have seen, size is relative. Apart from a limited number of firms that are giants by any standards, there are no absolutes. One may position oneself, legitimately and honestly, wherever is most advantageous. It must be determined which is the most appropriate to any particular circumstance.

The *small* syndrome might include words like: 'initiative', 'enterprise', 'human', 'friendly'; be defined as having concern for individual staff and customers, able to react quickly, highly motivated to good service, craftsmen, having an old-fashioned quality. But it may also mean old fashioned, short of money, lacking the will or resources to change, poorly organized, less reliable, unable to obtain the modern technologies necessary to create certain new products and services.

The *large* syndrome on the other hand may have as many pluses and minuses. It may mean advanced, efficient, well controlled, reliable, benefiting society by harnessing new technologies for making better products ('Progress,' says General Electric, 'is our most important product'), international, dynamic.

It may also mean autocratic, impersonal, slow to move, conservative, cautious, too powerful – able to manipulate governments, markets, and consumers alike.

Within our daily experience will be organizations that fit each one of these four profiles.

Even accepting that one tries, as the song says, to 'accentuate the positive, eliminate the negative' – which itself demands purposeful action neglected by many organizations – we must still ask whether it is better to attach oneself to the positive, *large* syndrome than to the positive, *small* one.

This is stated because too often there is the automatic assumption that the modern company should try to look as large as possible. From some points of view this may be so. Shareholders and bank customers like the maximum resources behind their money. But the same person, as a consumer, may feel differently.

It is hard to establish criteria. One clue lies in the sophistication of the product or service. Because it is widely thought that large organizations have large resources, they seem to be in the best position to produce obviously sophisticated products, and to know all there is to know about new technologies. This applies to the aircraft industry for example. But smaller firms can produce aircraft. Because they are small, such companies may give more personal attention, have more craftsmen, and fewer instruments of

British Rail: trains, stations, ships, freight, uniforms, posters, signs, carpets, curtains, place settings, design manual. All excellent design but no substitute for good management. Designers: Design Research Unit. It is interesting to compare it with Canadian National (lower right), whose design is also much admired.

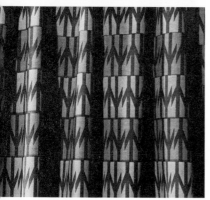

automation, and thereby actually be better people from whom to buy relatively simple aircraft.

In the automotive industry, attitudes are exactly reversed. For various reasons, the bigger company is thought the best to supply a relatively simple car; but the romance, the specialization, and the sophistication enjoyed by car enthusiasts may be thought to flow from companies with smaller production runs. In this field any required technical advance is seen as sufficiently established to be within the competence of small units, also it may be thought less vital than the engineering craftsmanship, which the smaller company is presumed to possess.

One can begin to see appropriate communication profiles being influenced by the product and market at which it is aimed. In any other industry the same principle will emerge. The degree of technological advance involved and expected is plainly relevant; so, at the other extreme, is the degree of craftsmanship or individual care expected.

The men's clothing industry is an example. Although an industry of large production units, every attempt is made to keep it looking small and personal. Despite the low price and high quality of ready-to-wear clothing, nearly half of all British men prefer to pay extra for suits made to measure. Since this figure includes the many thousands of suits which are assembled from precut pieces and sold by the retail clothing chains, it shows a desire for the luxury of personal attention.

This industry reveals other interesting attitudes. One tends to think that traditional firms which, in one's mind's eye are probably relatively small, are best for traditional materials. Coupled with this appears to be a belief in specialization. The preference for traditional materials, while it dies hard, can be altered and newer materials can take their place. But one might expect the best newer materials to come from larger firms.

This illustrates a polarization of attitudes within the same industry. It suggests that manufacturers will be wise to take note of prevailing attitudes to their industry, and to pinpoint with care the attitudes to their particular product types.

This can vary extremely from market to market. The Scotch whisky trade, dominated by the vast Distillers Corporation, skilfully manages to couple both a sense of absolute product constancy within any one brand (an advantage normally attached to large firms with good quality control), with the feeling that Scotch whisky is distilled by craftsmen in the Scottish highlands. This sense of centuries-old, personal craftsmanship is important to whisky.

Aware of this, a designer from London once went to Dublin and advised a distillery in Ireland that it should do more to communicate this personal involvement in whiskey distilling. 'Good God,' replied the distiller, 'that's just what we're trying to escape. Our trouble is that half the whiskey drunk in Ireland is all too personally distilled ' They needed to tell people that their brand of whiskey was bottled in the distillery which, because it was large, had the quality-control systems to ensure the product was reliable.

So we learn that an essential criterion must be the market itself. In many fields craftsmanship, because it reflects a quality thought rare, is a precious attribute. But, because craftsmanship is associated most naturally with traditional materials and methods, it is thought the prerogative of smaller firms. Craftsmen are disappearing as older methods are dying out. Complex modern industry demands the skills not of one man working with his hands but those of an organization of cerebral talents. The true craftsman is replaced by the team professional. In some situations, the bespectacled team of modern professionals can be seen as highly desirable, and a company with such a team can be seen as the one to buy from and deal with. This depends on the sophistication of the product in question.

The traditional virtue of craftsmanship has become an asset small firms can often claim and use to advantage. It fits readily into the small business syndrome and may therefore be readily accepted by the public. Indeed, so important may the virtue be thought, that it could influence companies to opt for the small rather than large profile. The larger company may find itself straining credulity if it makes what is essentially a 'small company' assertion.

Sometimes the large organization can successfully grasp the small-company virtues. Wilkinson Sword is an example. Makers of a modern disposable product, the name has become synonymous with high-quality razor blades.

By virtue of its name, which the company most judiciously decided to use even though swordmaking is now a modest part of its large business, Wilkinson Sword has managed to invest its mass-produced, mass-market razor blades with the quality of craftsmanship. Heavy television advertising for blades is focused almost entirely on swords. The commentary explains, 'Behind the Wilkinson Sword blade are centuries of craftsmanship in fine steel.' The name and the link, however tenuous, between the steel of a sword and the steel of a razor blade, have enabled the company to exploit the craftsmanship claim more often excluded and inappropriate to the larger and newer companies.

This is an interesting and apparently effective example of how a large industrialized organization has captured and used a 'small business' attribute. There are many similar examples of large organizations trying to do the same, particularly with the 'friendliness' attribute of smaller companies. Large companies are often thought impersonal, and it is not surprising that they try to combat this. Some do it by pretending to be smaller than they really are. Others, by making sure that people figure in all their advertisements and promotion matter.

Avis Rent-a-Car is an example of a brilliant exploitation of market position. Being only second biggest, it has attached to itself the virtue and necessity of smallness (though in fact it is also very large). Its 'we try harder' theme – human, frank, modest, service-oriented, like the garage around the corner –

by implication labels the market leader as too big to care for customers. Being self-critical, Avis gains sympathy.

Sears Roebuck, with 6000 stores in the US, plays it both ways. When research showed they were thought too remote (ironically because they had built their business serving remote areas by mail order), they set out to be seen as friendlier. They stress the fact that 'wherever you go Sears is only twenty miles away', and they humanize and simplify their image. However, when the company sells expensive hi-fi equipment it takes pains to lose that folksiness and establish on the product itself that it is made by 'a subsidiary of General Dynamics' with all the advanced technological know-how this infers.

An unusual approach was taken by United Airlines in a recent press advertisement which tried to straddle the almost contradictory thoughts. 'In a big country,' they said, 'it makes sense to fly the big airline.' That, as we've seen, is a clear statement of one position. But to counteract its possible consequences, a subsidiary slogan invoked people to 'Fly the friendly skies of United.' A third still smaller catchline asked, 'If they're so big, how-come they're so nice?'

That last question pinpoints the communication problem which United recognized and many companies would do well to face. There are important implications here for smaller firms too. To the extent that the large company successfully exploits both traditional craftsmanship and friendliness from the arsenal of the smaller company, it has deprived the smaller company of an advantage. The smaller company is more vulnerable and must fight back as it can.

All this has direct relevance to the design of corporate identities. Research has shown many times that abstract symbols can, among other things, be seen as representing a large or a small firm. The designer can influence people's impression of the company this way. The choice of typography can also influence attitudes in the same way. It is a generalization, but sometimes the use of all capital letters for a namestyle can convey ideas of formality, stiffness, and authoritarianism. There are numerous examples of companies changing their namestyle to use lighter upper- and lower-case letters for just this reason – to soften and humanize the organization. Van Gelder Papier and Albert Heijn in the Netherlands are instances. Dresdner Bank in Germany is another. In the UK (Lyons Bakery, in particular) and the US there are many others.

Some people, notably old-style advertising men, put a premium on impact. But is it really better to say the wrong things with force than to say the right things quietly? This is a permanent problem faced by corporate identity designers, but is by no means irreconcilable. Designing a visual identity scheme, designers are often put in the position of attempting to convey appropriate qualities for an organization with the right degree of modesty, dignity, or sophistication, while at the same time making sure that the design has impact. While complete visibility is certainly necessary, it is not overpoweringly important. Furthermore, visibility is easy to accomplish, as any designer knows. In total terms, it should seldom become a requirement that overwhelms others of a less tangible, though no less essential, nature.

There are enough examples of small firms that have made their mark with effective visual communications to encourage everyone.

Elkes Biscuits although the largest private cake and biscuit manufacturer in the UK, was small in comparison with the powerful United Biscuits, Associated Biscuits, or Westons. Their strategy was to coordinate all their packaging and other manifestations, projecting one name as strongly as possible. Their intentions: to see themselves and influence others to see them, as a large company.

At the other extreme is an English paint firm, again one of the larger private companies, but small and vulnerable in a field dominated by ICI and other large public concerns.

Hadfields, 130 years old, had been mainly concerned with the industrial and contract side of the paint business and, as so often happens, had found itself in the position of meeting individual specifications, so that it had 200 brand names and 7000 products. Predictably, the big battalions were forcing Hadfields to look for business in difficult, shrinking markets, and to face a dwindling profit situation. A new managing director, Wilfred Cass, was called in, and at once saw corporate identity work as a fundamental part of marketing strategy. 'I thought we needed a new image the day after I arrived,' he is reported to have said.

His strategy, rather than attempting to look large, was to emphasize the virtue of relative smallness. Wolff, Olins, the London designers, were appointed. They created a mascot for the company – a fox – to appear in different postures (running along the side of a vehicle, asleep on a doormat, sitting on paint cans). 'Wherever Hadfields went,' explained Mr Cass, 'the fox would go too.' The fox's paws appear on wet-paint-signs, on a press release with a message bubble coming from its mouth, and in 20 different positions on 20 different letterheads. Why 20 letterheads? The company has a small advertising budget and the effort has been made to make each letterhead a fresh advertisement. More importantly, the endless movement and variation stresses the vitality of the company.

The fox was chosen, according to the designers,

> because it represented ideas of quickness, intelligence and alertness and would (subconsciously or otherwise) contrast with the monolithic image of ICI.

Thus, Hadfields had elected, positively, to exploit the syndrome of virtues attributed to small business in its efforts to compete with the giants.

These were only part of the Hadfields' revolution. New products were introduced, paint cans were rationalized, old brand names were phased out and replaced by the corporate name to maximize impact.

Refreshingly inventive, the new scheme can leave no one in doubt that the

This paint company, founded in 1840, attributed to itself the small-company qualities (when it undertook a corporate identity programme recently) – flexibility, humour, speed. The fox is used in many ways, to keep contact with the company fresh. Design by Wolff, Olins.

145

company is revitalized, enterprising, and looking for business. But it must be emphasized that this vital design scheme is not for a moment seen as a substitute for good products. No company, and particularly no small company, will survive that way. Good product development had provided Hadfields with a new acrylic paint which gave them a base for sound marketing action, of which effective communication was seen as a central part. At the end of a year the new product sales were 300 per cent over target. Mr Cass asked:

> Can you be sure which part is bringing home the bacon? You must get it all right. You'll have more success if everything is consistent.

These two cases illustrate that the small company has communication needs at least as great as those of larger organizations. It suggests, too, that policies in this field need to be thought through with precision and woven into the heart of the company. Further, it is precisely because the larger organizations are becoming so concerned to project themselves favourably, that smaller firms must pay more attention to the subject.

As a salutary note, it is worth mentioning a recent study conducted by Professor Howard Perlmutter, until recently lecturing in Geneva and now at the Wharton School of Finance, Pennsylvania. He sees the world in 20 years' time dominated by 300 monster international companies with worldwide manufacturing and distribution facilities controlled by multinational teams of executives. Under them, he sees a mass of medium-sized organizations which will be 'the natural prey for the leviathans'. Swimming around the leviathans and their victims will be:

> shoals of small, fast fish – mounting guerilla raids on key markets, bringing out new products to fill the gaps, and living off their wits and their ability to react instantly to any shift in the balance of power.

This striking contrast between large and small, this polarization of industry, appears probable even though government attitudes in most countries seem confused on the subject. (In England there is both a Monopolies Commission to prevent firms getting too big and an Industrial Reorganization Corporation to help big firms get bigger.) The US Anti-trust Laws, which effectively limit the market share of any company below 50 per cent of the total, also have the effect of forcing the large corporations to look for growth internationally. There is little doubt that, as Perlmutter forecasts, a small number of mammoth firms will emerge to operate internationally. This means that the pressures on smaller firms will not decrease, and that they not only need to have a very clear understanding of their role to survive, but must exploit it and make it known to the full.

REFERENCES

1. *The Sources of Invention*, Macmillan, 1961.

13

Time, and the need to look forward

An essential ingredient of corporate identity considerations is time. It takes time to discuss the proper path to follow, time to implement, and time to take effect. One is trying to express the character of an organization to suit future conditions. In the period of only a few years, both the organization itself and the climate in which it operates will alter. The corporate identity, once established, will be expected to work effectively for a number of years.

Milner Gray says, 'We used to think a corporate identity should last for ever. Now we'd say ten years.' Wim Crouwel, partner in Amsterdam's Total Design, puts this at the maximum. Admittedly, cases vary. We've seen how some organizations can afford to be much more flexible in their approach than others. Further, a corporate identity, once set, can be modified. Of essence, it needs to be a dynamic, growing aspect of business, like any other function.

Therefore, a long look forward is required before important corporate identity change is introduced. It is astonishing how few companies or individuals are prepared to do this. There seems to be a psychological block which prevents it: a fear maybe, or at least suspicion of long words and science fiction.

In fact, serious attempts are now being made to understand the underlying trends in society and business, and to predict possible future developments. The best known is Herman Kahn's work for the Hudson Institute's Commission on the year 2000, sponsored by the American Academy of Arts and Sciences and supported by the Corning Glass Foundation and the Carnegie

Corporation, from which this chapter draws some guidelines. There are an increasing number of others: Battelle Memorial Institute, Stanford Research Institute, the Ford Foundation (with a body called Resources for the Future, Inc.), and OECD. In France, the Bureau d'Informations et de Prévisions Economiques, owned by the French Government and 50 big industrial companies, have drawn up long-range technological forecasts. In 1967, 70 scientists, engineers, and businessmen met in Oslo to inaugurate International Future Research.

This urge to look ahead has been going on a long time, as the examples of H G Wells, J B S Haldane, Bertrand Russell, and others testify. Even without the more recent methods of analysis and postulation, the degree of accuracy was impressive. In 1920 *Scientific American* forecast the coming 75 years. More than half their predictions were proved correct in 16 years. In 1945 Arthur Clarke forecast communication satellites in detail. The scale and pace of change in our world gives this whole approach to the future a new impetus and urgency. Indeed, few factors are more important than the acceleration of the rate of change. Examples abound to demonstrate this. A simple one: it took 1000 years or more, to go from the ability to travel 15 mph to 50 mph; say 60 years to go from that to 400 mph; just 20 years to hit speeds of 3000 mph. And now Dr Barnes Wallis is predicting aircraft with speeds of 25,000 mph. Herman Kahn calls this 'doubling time'. While the rate of acceleration doesn't increase indefinitely, it is sufficiently sharp and widespread to command the attention of any man taking decisions about the future, as is every big corporate identity decision.

A complicated chart on 'the rate of increase of operating energy in particle accelerations', published in *Daedalus 1962* shows the same thing. It shows a fivefold energy growth between 1930 and 1940; nearly a tenfold growth between 1940 and 1950, and almost a hundredfold growth between 1950 and 1960.

This energy revolution underlies a great part of the technological activity and possibility of modern life. Coupled with it must be what the science correspondent John Davy called 'the second truly fundamental revolution', namely the application of energy to processing information and data. He wrote:

> There can be little doubt that our technological evolution up to the end of the century will be centrally concerned with working out the consequences of information handling techniques. . . .

It has been said elsewhere in this book, that the amount of knowledge in the world is doubling every three years. Accurate in detail or not, the relevance of this to corporate communications, internal no less than external, is apparent.

These two developments (energy and information) have been quoted both for their own importance, and to stress the rate of change which it would be foolish to ignore. There must be very few businesses that can automatically expect to remain as they are today. Still fewer that can hope their audiences will not alter.

Without attempting to be definitive, this chapter will briefly outline some developments that may cause a reexamination of prevailing attitudes to specific corporate identity situations. All that is attempted in this book is to indicate areas of thought.

Many of the trends are already here, and a number have already been mentioned. Marshall McLuhan's analysis of media is an example. Controversially, he pointed out:[1]

> Societies have always been shaped more by the nature of the media by which men communicate than by the content of the communication.

Specifically, he claims:

> The alphabet and print technology fostered and encouraged a fragmenting process, a process of specialism and detachment. Electric technology [on the other hand] fosters and encourages unification and involvement.

McLuhan believes:

> It is impossible to understand social and cultural changes without a knowledge of the workings of media.

We see the impact of telephone, TV, and communication satellites clearly already. We see them unify and involve people. The interdependence of people brought about by modern electronics is manifest even when we don't see it.

This increase in involvement has been mentioned earlier in this book in another context, when McLuhan's theory of 'implosion' was described. Through TV, the whole world is brought to us and bears in on us. We are genuinely shocked by the assassination of a civil rights leader in Memphis or a maimed child in Saigon – events far removed from our own circle. Equally, we are open to the whole world: 250 million people watched Manchester United football team play Benfica at Wembley Stadium.

People want this involvement. It is impossible to contemplate corporate communications without being aware of the difference this makes to the relationship between any organization and its public. To look on TV as an entertainment medium, with bits of news and compulsory religion thrown in is to miss the point. It has become man's link with the world, and, to an extent, with other men.

We have seen how 'electric speed' permits anywhere to be the centre. This may affect companies of all kinds in several ways: first, their own organization may alter; second, the relationships between head offices and branches or subsidiaries may change; third, the buying power of customers may move elsewhere; fourth, local competition will increase; fifth, nationalism as a business concept will surely wane. Recognition of this basic concept of 'electric speed' may be one reason why US companies have moved so rapidly in Europe. Servan-Schreiber wrote,[2] 'Only the Americans have exploited the logic of the Common Market.' He attaches profound importance to the consequences. With a few exceptions, it cannot be said that British or other European firms or governments have learnt much about this yet.

Developments in industry have been forecast by many. In his book *The Reforming of General Education*, Daniel Bell uses the term 'post-industrial' to describe the next step in industrial evolution. He sees the trend like this: from a pre-industrial to an industrial society (basically production-oriented); from that to an 'advanced' society (a marketing-oriented consumer society); from that to 'post-industrial'. Servan Schreiber thinks that the US is becoming a post-industrial society and, as US business moves into Europe and invests in the modern growth areas, it will become different in kind from European business.

He describes the post-industrial society as having an industrial revenue fifty times greater than that of the pre-industrial period. He says most economic activity will have left the primary (agriculture) and secondary (production) sectors and will have reached a third and fourth stage (sectors and services). To some extent this trend is already clear. The most advanced companies are predominantly service-oriented. This, too, has direct relevance to questions of corporate identity.

The shift in gross national product (GNP) in the US towards service companies is most marked, and is certain to grow. In manufacturing organizations, service has become an integral part of the effective system of marketing. Nowhere is the wisdom of attempting to understand and legislate for the future clearer than here. In corporate identity terms, to neglect the benefits of one's service in favour of other attributes may be wrong. In government terms, to legislate against service organizations and to favour manufacturing, seems either an attempt to turn the clock back or a misreading of the undeniable trends in industry and society. Service is bound to be increasingly important to prosperity.

Daniel Bell claims that another characteristic of the post-industrial society is that private enterprise will have ceased to be the main source of technical and scientific action. This is an important thought and points to the increasing scale of finance necessary to back research projects. Already the Government pays for nearly two-thirds of the $25,000 million spent on research and development in the US. (Private industry does three-quarters of it, but the US Government pays for it.)

In the future, claims Bell, supported by Herman Kahn of the Hudson Institute, cybernetics will control the majority of industry. Although there are still clerks making manual entries in ledgers, already we've seen computers taking over clerical work, taking hold of complex industrial processes, and accelerating the whole process of production design, development, and tooling-up. Hours of drudgery spent selecting and specifying materials, producing and checking drawings, and setting up production programmes will be removed.

In consumer terms, cybernetics will be no less dramatic. Bankers today envisage the decline of cash, and certainly plan far-reaching computer services.

This alarms Servan-Schreiber. He points out that US companies lead in just these modern fields. In 1963 he reckoned US industry controlled 50 per cent of the semi-conductor business in Europe, 80 per cent of computers, and 95 per cent of integrated circuits: all advanced technologies on which Europe will depend.

The main factors of progress in a post-industrial society, claims Bell, will depend on the education and technical innovation put at its service. Kahn predicts a 'rapid improvement in educational institutions and learning techniques'.

This must be so. It bears on the modern corporation, government, or other institutions in many ways. For one thing, there is no doubt that education will be a primary factor in business growth. Every company must have sophisticated measures for improving the knowledge of its staff and executives and be prepared to replace out-of-date with new skills. The rash of new methods, materials, processes, and ideas furnish a stark choice for all business: keep up or fall behind.

A relevant aspect of this is that the audiences at which any company is aiming, both within and outside the organization are going to be increasingly literate. Successful communications will be those which, in all directions, at all levels are reconciled to this inevitability. The increase in literacy in the last thirty years has not been universally recognized by employers.

There is another implication, as recent student and other political demonstrations show. While problems become more complex, demanding more skilled and expert knowledge to be resolved, the literate public wants to partake increasingly in the decision-making process. No longer is there the automatic assumption of superiority at the centre or top which characterized political and industrial life for many years. Realistic business will shape its organization and communication policies accordingly, sharing decisions, training others lower down to take decisions (unions no less than management), then seeing that these decisions are communicated intelligently throughout the organization.

A study carried out at Princeton University showed that employees could put to best use three types of information: First, anything giving them a better insight into their work and the work of others in the firm. Second, anything which gave them a sense of belonging to the firm. Third, any information which improved their sense of status and importance as individuals in the firm.

This trend will have a bearing on design standards. It is widely thought that the public is visually illiterate. Every designer has heard clients criticize his work for being 'too good for the market'. This remark is usually uninformed, an expression of excessive caution. On the whole acceptable levels are miles ahead of the level client companies insist on, as the success of many foreign, well-designed articles indicates.

There is evidence enough to encourage one to hope that an appreciation of good design is yet another widespread and rapid development. According to Victor Papanek, Chairman of Industrial and Environmental Design at Purdue University, people are being exposed to far more symbolic language, for example, than ever before, and this has increased visual understanding. As evidence of this, too, he cites the way people can distinguish one colour from another. He states that the ability to distinguish colour has gone from 200 colours to 800 in 10 years (as ink, paint, print, and textile manufacturers have mastered the technologies of colour formation and reproduction). There is no doubt whatever that the universal enjoyment of colour has increased dramatically.

As design becomes a more significant factor in marketing, there's no reason to think this trend to more design awareness among the public will diminish. Thus, in shaping their visual identities, companies looking forward can, with confidence, set their standards higher than they might think proper today. Companies which fail to raise standards will be judged adversely.

Daniel Bell also characterized the post-industrial society as being one in which 'time and space won't be important to communication'. (Back to McLuhan.)

He claims that the variation in a post-industrial society between high and low incomes will be less than we now know in an industrial society. This is evident enough in Europe already. Incomes, of course, are expected to rise more or less continuously. So are government spending, taxes, and the GNP.

Herman Kahn, in the first volume of the studies done at the Hudson Institute on this subject, postulates all these figures in detail for a number of countries.[3]

All these theories concern the so-called 'post-industrial society'; it has been suggested that in only thirty years the US, Japan, Canada, and Sweden will have reached these conditions fully.

By the year 2000, Britain is seen as likely to have increased its GNP fivefold since 1950. On a chart it is clustered with Germany and France, but a long way below the US, USSR, and Japan. (A medium forecast puts the *per capita* GNP of Britain at £2554 by the year 2000, compared with £751 in 1965. The rise of Japan, by all calculations, is startling. The competitive aspect, as well as the wisdom of establishing good communications with Japanese industry may be commented on.

The indication is that the gap between rich and poor countries will widen, with Europe positioned between the most advanced and the backward countries. Not only may this view influence trading and investment decisions, but one can see it influencing communication and identity policies.

Other developments that are envisaged by the Hudson Institute include, 'an erosion of middle-class, work-orientated, achievement-orientated values'. Sapping at the basic structure of Western society and industry, this development, were it to occur, could exert enormous influence on corporate life and certainly on its communications. People will have more money, more leisure, less need to work (by the end of the century a working year of 147 days at 7 hours a day is envisaged in the US).

An 'erosion' of 'national interest values' is thought possible. It's happening. Increasingly 'sensate', secular, humanist, self-indulgent criteria may become central. Already one sees ample evidence, enough for every executive to know that the standards applied to the discipline of work, for example, are quite unlike those that were suitable even a few years ago.

This is no academic point. Recruiting and maintaining an effective workforce, trained in new skills, is bound to be a preoccupation of management. And this is emphasized at a time when the potential fears of automation could flare into a new Luddite resistance to change. The most competent industrial relations are required in the foreseen future.

Because they influence the kind of design needed to communicate with audiences, sensate attitudes should be described. Philosophers, while not always in agreement, have a remarkable similarity of language. Kahn quotes Sorokin, Spengler, Toynbee, Schubart, and others.

The three stages they speak of include:

1. *Ideational* – revealed, charismatic, certain, dogmatic, mystic, intuitive, infallible, religious, supersensory, unworldly, salvational, spiritual, absolute, supernatural, moral, emotional.
2. *Sensate* – empirical, pragmatic, operational, practical, worldly, scientific, sceptical, tentative, fallible, sensory, materialistic, mechanical, relative, agnostic, empirically or logically verifiable.
3. *Late sensate* – cynical, disillusioned, nihilistic, chaotic, blasé, transient, superficial, weary, sophistic, atheist, trivial, changeable, meaningless, alienated, expedient.

The view tends to be that Europe is in a late sensate stage. Certainly one can see evidence of this in society. How widespread it is remains another question. One wonders whether the students revolts should be described in these words; whether the 'Swinging London' scene is just a cheerful, optimistic expression of new freedom or the sign of disillusioned cynicism. It could be that the pop scene is essentially a conformist outlet for basic uncertainties about society, or it might, *in extremis*, deteriorate into Trotskyist revolt, or drug-taking and withdrawal from it all.

A culture is most deeply held at its zenith by an élite which up to now has usually been an educated or dominant middle and upper class. The élite in this sense today may be quite different – the 'young who understand'.

This particular prognostication of the future has been dwelt on for several reasons. It is impossible to communicate effectively without knowing what basic attitudes are influencing one's audience. Something new is going on that must be understood. Within any society, each of the three stages described is likely to be present. It is highly relevant to our purpose to assess which characteristics are most likely to be current among the audience we are aiming at. One can imagine frequent occasions when the same company wishes to appeal to more than one group. Herbert Johnson, the London hatter, makes hats for army officers and for latterday squires' wives; he also makes them for Nureyev and the Beatles, as well as the derivatives, as it were, of both groups. How should that company's message differ to suit such diverse audiences?

Different countries can be in different stages of development at the same time. However indestructible are the ideas of Britain as a conservative country, mightn't it be right too that it *appears* to be a far later sensate society than, say, the United States or even much of Europe. This may explain some of its weaknesses if not its strengths. This difference between countries is clearly worth identifying by anyone seriously interested in effective international communications.

One possible development is a swing away from a prevailing culture towards another. For Britain a swing from a late sensate stage, if that is where it now stands, towards an earlier, more puritan, moral, strict, absolute, standard has been forecast by Sir Paul Reilly, director of the Council of Industrial Design, and cannot be ruled out.

This chapter has not so far concerned itself with the many wondrous technical developments in the next thirty years. One is relevant now: 'the pill'. According to Ronald Clark (writing in *The Director*, May 1968), the production of a totally satisfactory birth control pill is only a few years away. This will be a development, he says:

> ... with implications as important as prehistoric man's change from a hunting to an agricultural society; it is certainly likely to give contemporary ideas of a so-called permissive society the air of a Methodist meeting.

Against this, it could be thought that too disintegrated a society would be impossible to govern, and this may impose its own restraints. Either way, the question is a critical one for the modern company to ponder.

It is forecast that the free market will play a diminished role compared to the public sector. In Britain already, government spends almost half the GNP. By taxation, nationalized industries, the Prices and Incomes Board, by backing major research projects, and in other ways, it has a sizeable say on what's left. It seems this trend is to continue. Between 1965 and 1969, the *Daily Telegraph* estimates, public investment in Britain will have risen 54 per cent, public expenditure by 40 per cent, taxes and subsidies by 57 per cent. This compares with an expected growth of private investment of 30 per cent.

Among many implications is the obvious need for industry to enjoy good relations with government; indeed to exert an influence on government. The implications run deeper and cast doubt on the continuity of the consumer society as we know it, or the sovereignty of consumer choice. This trend will influence design. The criterion of effectiveness could shift from the sales and profit which good design generates, to the money it saves. Cost, particularly under socialism, may conceivably become more important than profit.

'Small World' is seen as another important trend. The idea is not new and needs no elaboration. It means that all our major competitors and markets will come to be next door. The Victorian notion of exports, of Conradian ships beating their way bravely to strange foreign ports, is a long time dying. The Hudson Institute couple with this 'very small world' as they put it, an increasing need for regional or worldwide control of arms, technology, pollution, trade, transportation, population, and resource utilization. They say that there is a basic long-term trend which should continue unless it is interrupted by one or more of the four horsemen of the Apocalypse. They describe this trend as towards:

1. Increasingly sensate cultures.
2. Bourgeois, bureaucratic, meritocratic, and democratic élites.
3. Accumulation of scientific and technological knowledge.
4. Institutionalization of change, especially research, development, and innovation.
5. Worldwide industrialization and modernization.
6. Increasing affluence and leisure.
7. Population growth.
8. Urbanism and, soon, the growth of megalopses.
9. Decreasing importance of primary and secondary occupations.
10. Literacy and education.
11. Increasing capacity for mass destruction.
12. Increasing tempo of change.
13. Increasing universality of this basic trend.

Unless there are dramatic or surprising events, they predict high growth rates in GNPs. (It has been observed that growing national wealth makes it possible to conceive very large social undertakings, and one wonders what these may be.) Increasing emphasis on 'meaning and purpose' is also foreseen. (Can industry identify with the community by helping to provide meaning and purpose? How will it fare if it can't?)

Also forecast is turmoil in new and industrializing nations; the potential rise of Japan to being the third largest power; further rises of Europe and China; emergence of new intermediate powers (maybe Brazil, Mexico, Pakistan, Indonesia, East Germany, or Egypt); some *relative* decline in the US and USSR; an absence of stark life-or-death political and economic issues in the old nations. On balance they expect the next thirty years will be mostly peaceful.

Surprisingly, they do not mention the continuing rise of large organizations. Yet, if we ask what future developments are likely, the rise of the multinational companies seems one of the most relevant. Robert Heller, editor of *Management Today*, reckons that the multinational corporations will be

IS THIS JUST ANOTHER FAD?

The big beret.

12s 6d.

12 Quant colours.

Enquiries
for Quant berets
to
39 Fitzroy
Square,
London W1.

MARY QUANT

Mary Quant, a big business expressed as a fresh, young, personal one; in the vanguard
of fashion yet with a long-lasting omnipresent identity.

'the dominant economic organization of the 1970s and beyond'. What exists at the moment, he believes, is the international group mostly controlled from one country, holding shares of the market in several other countries.

Various pressures, as well as natural evolution, will force internationalization. Not least are the anti-trust or anti-monopoly laws evident in many countries that effectively limit the size of any company's domestic market. Diversification provides some answers, but even this has politically acceptable limits. The pattern of the biggest companies appears to be that most have substantial international activities. Half the top 100 companies have a quarter of their assets or sales outside their domestic country of origin. Perhaps because their own markets are smaller, European companies are notably stronger in this sense. Volkswagen has 67 per cent of its sales outside Germany; BP 89 per cent; ICI 50 per cent; Hoescht 46 per cent; Renault 42 per cent; Hawker Siddeley 56 per cent; BAT earns 88 per cent of its profits abroad.

In general, such big European companies tend to have fewer assets abroad and greater exports than their US rivals, though there are outstanding exceptions. Nestlé, for instance, has only four of its 198 factories in Switzerland.

The likely development, politicians permitting, is that the pattern will move from exports to local assembly and to local manufacturing, with all the problems this entails.

Up to now, with few exceptions, this international growth has been colonial in character. The heart of empire has sent out its colonizers, and colonies have sent back their tribute. In this sense American companies have been far more active than the European giants. A significant part of the equity of Shell, Unilever, and Philips, all European companies, for example, is held in the US. Sir Francis de Guingand, former chairman of Carreras in the UK (cigarettes like Rothmans, Peter Stuyvesant, Guards, Piccadilly; cigars like Schimmelpenninck; tobacco; and, through Alfred Dunhill Ltd, lighters and pipes) claims that his company never take more than a 50 per cent stake when it starts in a new country. 'I feel it's only right that the locals should share the successes,' he says. It is also known that they have been well accepted wherever they've gone because local government, bankers, customers, and workers alike can identify the growth of the business with the growth of their economy. Carreras is a part of the South African Rembrandt tobacco organization. Significantly, while the South Africans hold only 22 per cent of the equity, they control 50 per cent of the votes. This suggests that while ownership may to some extent be local, control by the parent may be maintained.

Professor Perlmutter's division of international corporations works like this. First, there is the 'ethnocentric' company. This has a powerful headquarters and complex manufacturing and marketing organization in the country of origin. Orders flow from the centre to subsidiaries. There tends to be a strong feeling that nationals from the home country are superior. He quotes:

> There's only one way to do things, and that's the way we do them in Hoboken (or London or Tokyo).

Subsidiaries are staffed with nationals from the home country.

Professor Perlmutter believes such companies will find it hard to transfer to the superleague of 300 giant companies which will dominate world business. His reasons: they find it difficult to respond quickly to local conditions, they are viewed with suspicion by host governments, and morale of local staff is low when the best jobs go to nationals from headquarters.

Companies in the second category, he thinks, will find it easier. These are 'polycentric' companies able to take decisions in different local markets where standards of performance can be determined locally and where they are identified with their markets.

Philips, Alcan, and Hoover are cited as such companies.

The 'blue chip' companies, according to Perlmutter, are in the third group. He calls them 'geocentric'. The geocentric corporation is complex and interdependent, with subsidiaries helping in making decisions, applying standards both universal and local.

The location of the headquarters is considered an accident of history. It can be altered to suit changing tax and corporation laws. The distinguishing characteristic of the geocentric company is the internationalism of its executives. It knows the home country does not possess a monopoly of men or ideas.

> A man's passport is of small importance compared to his abilities and his willingness to serve wherever the corporation sends him.

IBM (whose World Trade organization functions as an entity outside the US), Royal Dutch/Shell, and Unilever, are good examples. Because they may herald the new dimension and standards of business performance, the corporate identity policy of each is considered in the next chapter.

The growing size of companies, particularly those that are structured to be really effective locally, has many implications. It means research to remain competitive, raising ever larger sums of money, probably specialization, certainly service, certainly design, communications, and corporate identity. It may mean mergers – one's corporate identity should be ready for the possibility. For the supplier company, it means larger orders from fewer clients. The supplier is more vulnerable to that extent. It also means continually raising the standards of competence and service. The larger companies are keenly aware of cost effectiveness, and demand high performance. At the same time, they want security, too. It would be wrong to assume that they are uninfluenced by a good reputation built not only from performance but also from effective communications. The executive in the big company can afford the comfort of security provided by dealing with the best-known firm in its field.

Companies which are both big and dynamic (not all are both) tend to be highly sophisticated in their image and communication policies. As they grow, so will competitors need to step up the calibre of *their* communications with *their* customers, trade, bankers, workers, and others.

This chapter has so far resisted the considerable temptation to dwell on some of the many exciting and provocative technological, biological, and social developments that have been forecast. Instead it has concentrated on a few of the considerations most likely to be relevant to people planning corporate identity activity. Companies must make their own assessments of their own future.

One or two final comments can be made about the future. The first is that future predictions almost always underestimate because they take little account of inventions not yet made. It seems though that one of the few certainties of the future is that in addition to the astonishing products already foreseen, there will be others still more impressive. Innovation can be counted on. If anyone in the last thirty years had looked ahead without reckoning on the possibility of new techniques, he would have underestimated badly the progress actually made.

We can think of many long-term projects quickly proved inadequate, from airport to highways, because of so-called 'responsible pessimism'. Coupled with this, must be repeated the astonishing acceleration of the rate of change we saw earlier. It's all happening now, and a great deal faster than we can appreciate. It would be foolhardy to neglect the fact. To base decisions which will work into this volatile future on situations prevailing today or even yesterday, would be equally short-sighted. Decisions concerning corporate identity are among them.

The purpose of this all-too cursory glance at a few possible developments in society, and of others mentioned throughout the book, is to stress that corporate identity work is inherently concerned with fitting the organization into a *future* situation. It can only be effective to the extent that the future is appreciated.

REFERENCES

1. *The Medium is the Message*, Penguin, 1968.
2. *The American Challenge*, Hamish Hamilton, 1968.
3. *The Year 2000*, Collier-Macmillan, 1968.

14

Should your identity be international or local?

In 1967 George Ball who, for five years, was Under-Secretary to the US Treasury, talked to the New York Chamber of Commerce about the multi-national corporation. He made the interesting point that while the structure of the multinational corporation is a modern concept,

> The nation state is a very old-fashioned idea and badly adapted to suit the needs of our present complex world. [Most nation states] are totally inadequate as economic units, too small to provide effective domestic markets. ... Unless we can make faster progress in modernizing the world's political structure, the multinational corporation may find itself increasingly harassed by obstacles and restrictions that will seriously reduce its potential.

He went on to discuss the fear some nations have of US dominance, the hypersensitiveness to colonialism of developing countries, and the difficult restrictions they place on foreign companies. To some extent these are questions that can be influenced by effective corporate communications.

How do companies that face these problems deal with them? This chapter will look at the policies of three giants whose leadership can be a guide to many.

No company in the world is more international than Unilever. Few are larger or continue to grow so continuously. Significantly, their communication attitudes are highly sophisticated, in the best sense, and abundantly illustrate the flaws in a lot of other vehemently held doctrines.

It is fashionable today to talk of 'global communications', of the need to establish a strong corporate identity. But what does Unilever, one of the most international and 'multinational' of companies, do? It is popular and easy to say that if a company works on the brand policy it has no need of corporate communications. But what about Unilever – the company that invented the brand theory and established its own marketing organization forty years before the idea became widespread? What do they do?

Their problems and their solutions are not the same as anyone else's. But it would be a mistake to move into the realms of international communication policies without looking at this gentle giant.

First, some facts. Unilever is, according to *Fortune* (1967), the seventh largest company in the world. Sales that year exceeded £2000 million ($4800 million). It started life as an international group when, in 1929, the Dutch Margarine Unie merged with the British Lever Brothers Limited.

Today it has 304,000 employees in more than 60 countries, and sells in many more. A far-sighted international policy has brought its rewards. Early to move into underdeveloped and developed countries alike, they now find no less than 36 per cent of their turnover coming from outside their original 'home' markets in Europe. They take pains to be apolitical, but there is little doubt that in some areas of the world their influence as a stabilizing force is considerable.

Unilever people like to say they have a 'vested interest in raising standards of living'. Their policies are decisively shaped to encourage local growth and to integrate their companies and activities into the local scene. The degree of their effectiveness is an example to industry everywhere. When the President of the Federal Republic of West Africa (Cameroun) opened a new Unilever palm oil mill in 1967 he said:

> The company is keenly aware of its social obligations. It already has to its credit praiseworthy achievements in the fields of health, educational and vocational training. . . . The confidence we have placed in you by granting you the status of a privileged partner in the development of our economy has thus been justified. . . . We hope that the moral credit and esteem which you enjoy among the people of West Cameroun will continue to grow.

The President's comment, in an age of often aggressive independence, speaks for Unilever's policies. Businessmen in their offices in London, New York, Paris, or Rotterdam may think Cameroun a too small and distant market to choose as an example. In fact, it is the degree of penetration (and the sincerity this implies) of the company's policies that make them so distinguished. And if this example is dismissed as an official pronouncement, let us quote a Nigerian manager who, speaking at a management course in England, said, 'United Africa Company [a Unilever subsidiary] has been both father and mother to my country.'

In Nigeria, the share of local management has advanced from 12 per cent

Chase Manhattan may fairly claim that corporate communications are effective when cartoons appear in kindly support of their theme. At right, appear examples of sales promotion items offered to customers as tokens of goodwill. Standards, running from architecture to cufflinks, are consistent and good.

THE CHASE MANHATTAN BANK, N.A.

"I hate to knock over Chase Manhattan, it's such a friendly bank."

to 50 per cent in 10 years. In East Africa generally 72 per cent of the company's management is indigenous. From Norway to New Zealand, from Turkey to Tunisia and Trinidad, the story is the same – of a company involved in its local environment with a remarkable degree of success. This success comes neither by accident nor automatically. Glance at any week in the diary of Unilever and notice courses, lectures, visits, and a very consistent programme of participation by management and personnel in local affairs of all kinds.

It is salutary to learn this. Many companies hoping to operate internationally – or even domestically – allocate little time or resource to anything outside the business. They think they have good reasons for not doing so, but the changing relationship of industry to society and, the increasing dependence on its environment of the modern corporation will expose them in time as short-sighted.

The companies that steamroller into other countries without so much as a change of gear will find the going harder and harder. Already there has been evidence of a growing resentment of this kind of overt invasion. Cleverer by far are the companies that take pains to become respected as local developments, giving as much as they take. True anywhere, this has special force in the emergent countries. Unilever, for all its sophisticated understanding of these problems, has itself been nationalized in Burma, Iraq, Egypt, and elsewhere. The dangers are there, and will remain for years to come.

The communication policies of Unilever are complicated in three ways. First, Unilever is a very large group and this, they recognize, imposes special responsibilities on them. Their more important activities are major news events. The financial results of the twin parent companies are used by economists, sociologists, the Press, and others for a number of purposes. The business is looked to by government, industry, and scientific, farming, cultural, and educational bodies for help and information. Unilever has to be careful to avoid monopoly situations (the true story is told of a Unilever company in South America that planned and created all the advertising for a competitor, to keep it in business).

Second, the group is international, in every respect. Unilever has always recognized the wide variations to be found in the world, and believed that local managers knew best how to deal with them. But as far back as 1942 its directors foresaw that in many countries where they operated they could expect growing nationalism. They saw, too, that the 'capitalist', 'free enterprise' or 'profit motive' systems would come under increasing attack. Big business, just because it was big, would be suspected. At that time, when throughout the world they were desperately caught up in the war, they determined to change their postwar PR policy. They created a 'long-term positive and progressive plan' which involved publishing much more information than ever before.

The group grew as a loose federation of companies, with a high level of local autonomy. They were primarily responsible to London or Rotterdam for their budgets, capital expenditures, and the appointments of senior managers. Only now are more executive powers moving to the centre. Today, for instance, they have six directors who are product group coordinators, with executive responsibility in most of Europe and an advisory role throughout the rest of the world.

Third, the Unilever twins are holding companies. They do not, in fact, manufacture or market products. Because these functions are performed by operating companies with varying names throughout the world and invariably under a strong brand identity for each product or range, the general consumer is not aware of being in close touch with Unilever. In 1948, for example, a public opinion poll showed that 85 per cent of the UK population had never heard of Unilever. Some of those who had heard of Unilever but knew little about it, nonetheless had a 'vague impression that Unilever was a large financial octopus and, because of its bigness, a bad thing'.

It was decided that, even it if were possible, the launching of a high-powered PR campaign to counter this ignorance would only increase suspicion. (This realistic appraisal echoes the theories expressed in chapter 3.) It was thought better to concentrate on what are called the 'opinion-moulders' – Members of Parliament, trade union officials, journalists, school teachers, university staff, civil servants, and others. Their own staff, too, should be better informed, they felt, and should be in a position to provide information about the company. Shareholders should know more. And they decided to give more educational help to young people.

This has all gone on deliberately for 20 years. The list of Unilever publications, ranging from the theory of network analysis to looking after teeth, is too long to describe. In Britain, in 1968, Unilever's Richard Wilson won 16 awards from the British Association of Industrial Editors. Their film library is extensive. In 1967 their more than 50 films were seen by 9 million people outside the company. They range from *Water in Biology* to *The Electronic Computer in Commerce*. The company is particularly concerned with education. A new series of beautifully produced booklets aims to help school children with their A-level exams. Titles include *The Chemistry of Proteins*, *The Physics of Chemical Structure*, *The Chemistry of Glycerides*, and others. Booklets and wall charts have been prepared for pupils in class; film strips for teachers.

Here is evidence of a company spending money to influence opinion gently by providing material help. There's no doubt the company has an eye on long-term recruitment. While many students view industry as a 'cold, hard rat-race' to be avoided, Unilever tells them of the 'intellectual challenge industry offers'.

This view is refreshingly at odds with the many companies who neglect the increasingly pressing problem of recruiting good-quality management and staff to face future conditions. The growth of automation means they need more specialist skills than ever before. They must have people who understand *how* to use computers.

United Africa Company's training manager wrote:

> A shortage of skilled manpower is a world problem. Even in highly-industrialised countries demand . . . far exceeds supply.

(He pointed out that in developing countries the problem is particularly serious. To meet it, Unilever in Africa has established a number of technical schools where, since 1954, nearly 3000 students have taken technical courses.)

This is a potential problem not seriously tackled by many companies which, believing in the 'brand' concept, have no corporate activity aimed at universities, schools, or anywhere else.

Despite their own spread of companies operating under different names, and with their own branded products, Unilever believes there is a need for corporate communication activity. For one thing, they think there is more chance of attracting graduates to join Unilever, as a socially conscious, advanced, and worldwide organization, than of persuading them to join Birds Eye or Omo, or Calvé. It sounds obvious, but many companies adhere to an opposite point of view.

Presenting a clear impression of Unilever is difficult. It was once said, 'Unilever has so many audiences it is difficult to stand in one relationship to them all.' Even so, in 1964 they decided to strengthen their corporate image. The reason, they say, was that:

> even in areas of informed opinion Unilever had no point of identification. This is good to have from an external point of view. And it's good internally – so that people can say 'that's us'.

A compass design had been used for some years, but they felt it was not used well nor was it worth using more strongly.

Here's how Unilever set about creating a new visual identity. They established a working party, consisting of the head of the Information Division in London, his opposite number, the head of public relations in Rotterdam, and a senior representative of the marketing division. Together they produced a brief, of little more than 1000 words, which stated: (a) the basic aim, (b) the nature of Unilever, (c) types of items to be covered, and (d) the desired company image.

It pointed out that, since manufacturing and marketing is done by subsidiary companies, Unilever itself needs no labels, shop fronts, factories, delivery vans or product advertising. But because it is a large organization it puts out a great deal of paper under the Unilever name. They felt they needed a symbol and a corporate style to unify this.

The image they want to project is that Unilever is *international* and *outward-looking*; its size inspires *confidence*; but the size must not imply heaviness. On the contrary, Unilever is always active and 'one jump ahead of most other people'. The company is *efficient*, *modern*, *well ordered*, run by people who take a pride in doing things well. It's a *human* business, a company you'd like to work in. It is *agreeable to deal with*. And it is *durable*, likely to last.

The working party decided to use outside consultants for this task because they felt the subject needed an objective viewpoint.

The brief was given to the designers (Design Research Unit in London) who, in time, presented six alternative designs (with one preference) first to the working party, then to the Unilever board's special committee. It is important to notice the weight of this committee. Essentially, it is the executive head of the group with powers delegated by the board for general formation and oversight of policy and day-to-day running of the business. It consists of the chairman of Unilever Limited (Lord Cole), the chairman of Unilever NV (Harold Hartog), and a vice-chairman of Unilever Limited (Dr E G Woodroofe).

Notice the stark contrast between the importance attached to this question in Unilever, and the inconsequential value given it by numerous other companies.

Preferred designs were submitted to the full board. Three representatives of the designers were present, with the three members of the working party. About two dozen people were there in all. The board was asked to vote in secret.

At the time of writing, the work is still going on. When it is complete, instructions and standards, carrying the chairman's authority, will be dispatched to all head office departments, and others using the new material. The design programme has taken longer, cost more, been more difficult than they expected, but it is still thought necessary.

Clearly, Unilever's attitude to corporate communication is of the most sophisticated, far-reaching and effective kind. The visual aspects are one part of the whole, but even so they are treated at the highest level. Expressions of the company are based on real policies, as thorough and appropriate in Thailand as in New York. The relationship between individual companies and the group has been thought through and established. While the group visual identity is going on, for example, Thames Board Mills, Unilever's giant UK papermaking firm, commissioned designers to conduct a similar study for itself. This, too, is seen as one aspect of corporate policy. When Thames Board Mills opened a new pulp and paper mill in Cumberland, the Prime Minister congratulated them on their 'progressive thinking' and on 'making full use of indigenous resources'.

While certain PR, employee-relation, and management functions are coordinated centrally, great emphasis is placed on the responsibility of individual companies to sell their products. The centre does nothing to interfere with this. Even though the central Unilever organization is strengthening its own expression, and transmits information about the parent company to its members abroad, it makes no attempt to communicate directly to outside audiences abroad. The local company is free to decide its own attitudes. The prime consideration is the individual business and the success of its operations.

Whether this freedom will remain wholly intact remains to be seen. Research has shown Unilever that, while an employee's first loyalty is to his local company, 'there is undoubtedly room for group loyalty'. The company has a programme of magazines, information bulletins, and courses, and in these and other ways helps inform staff of the group's activities and build recognition of the greater organization to which they belong. It is probable that the prevailing philosophy will continue in principle.

We started by saying that Unilever's answers do not necessarily suit everyone's problems. But they serve to show that subtle relationships may exist. They show a successful method of operating internationally, and a profound respect for the people who comprise their working strength, and so provide lessons for others to learn.

We looked at Unilever, as one of the world's most international companies, and hoped to learn from it. So one may. But, to emphasize the lack of firm rules, it is interesting to see what Royal Dutch/Shell does. Here is another Anglo-Dutch enterprise, the fourth largest industrial enterprise in the world. Selling one-seventh of the free world's oil (investing £600 million ($1440 million) a year on exploration and research), with 180,000 employees in 500 companies, it is bigger than and as international as Unilever. Yet its policies are almost the opposite.

While Unilever has built itself on a *brand* philosophy with a supporting corporate identity so slight that this now needs strengthening, Shell has consistently projected a strong *corporate* look which is much the same everywhere. Most of its brands are product dominated by and obviously tied to Shell.

While advanced companies are now moving towards tying together their sprawling activities by establishing an office of corporate identity, Shell has had a design office for its 'visible manifestations' since the 1930s.

This office, charged with the responsibility for seeing that the Shell identity is the same everywhere, has also been concerned with keeping the visual identity up to date. While outsiders may be unaware of change, the company has been moving forward steadily for many years. For fifty years it has been using the Shell pecten, and the red and yellow colours, though the precise details of each have been evolving all the time.

Only recently, although armed with all most companies require (design manuals, films, film strips, firm standards, and good organization for implementation), Shell has retained Raymond Loewy's Paris office to undertake a wholesale re-evaluation of the subject. Why?

One reason they give is that they recognize the changing role of the oil companies, their changing problems and changing opportunities. Although sometimes slow to move, Shell is very concerned with the future, and wants to be well placed to deal with it.

Their international aspects pose particular problems and their point of view is relevant to consideration of their image. Always vulnerable to the ambitions of emerging countries, fearful of nationalization, an obvious target for taxation, they find themselves sitting in the middle of rising markets, but hampered by political considerations on all sides. David Barron, the chairman of Shell Transport and Trading (which, with Royal Dutch Petroleum, owns all companies in the Royal Dutch/Shell Group) told the British Institute of Management in 1967 that:

> In choosing the countries in which to put our money we must look not only at the likely commercial return on investment but also at the attitudes towards foreign capital displayed by the Government.

He points out, by the way, that governments of industrialized countries are often no less restrictive in their attitudes to private enterprise.

These attitudes can hurt Shell, but they don't do much good to the underdeveloped countries either. Another senior executive, C C Pocock, the coordinator for the Western hemisphere, has said he fears the poorer countries may get poorer in the sense that investment will go where it is treated best. He said:

> It is better to get 7 or 8 per cent in a country that sticks by the rules and is sympathetic towards investment on a continual basis than to try to get 20 per cent return in a country that may change its rules, expropriate, or restrict the flexibility of the company.

Clearly the relationship between the group and the 100 countries in which it operates are of fundamental importance. The point of this concern was evident in 1967 when Shell's operations were made more difficult by the Suez Canal being closed, the Arab embargo on sales to the UK and US, interrupted supplies from Nigeria, and devaluation. In 1968 Shell installations in Biafra were invaded and burnt by demonstrating mobs. Small wonder the group is now trying to find means of assessing and quantifying political risks.

This great involvement in the world may cause Shell to find itself a victim of its own highly developed and universal corporate identity. The Shell image shows itself, in survey after survey, to be among the two or three best known in the world. Indeed, in Shell, now strongly regionalized with autonomous companies, one of the few mandatory requirements is that the company looks the same worldwide. The more people travel (and a part of the oil business is largely about travel), the better this is.

But three sets of questions spring to mind at once:

1. Can any company as international as Shell afford to be 'foreign' to most people? Does one have to accept the obvious dangers in order to have a 'global' image? In view of the dangers, is it wise to have such universal identity? Do customers travel as much as the Shell executives who frame the policies?
2. With some retail outlets in the world, one may say that Shell is uniquely

placed to benefit from the massive swing in marketing emphasis from manufacturing to distribution. Is the inseparable corporate/brand image the best to sell products at a retail level? The 'after-markets' (sales, mostly at petrol stations, of packaged goods ranging from motor oil to flykiller) are an underdeveloped side of any oil company's business, although international conferences on this subject are held annually by Shell. At present the packaging has a very strong corporate look, and for the layman, it is often difficult to distinguish one product from another quickly. Wouldn't more emphasis on products be helpful to sales? Would this mean weakening the corporate image?

3. The variations Shell has in its images are between operations, the aviation side looks different in detail from the automotive business. Shell chemical is different again. If variations are required, is this a logical split, from the point of view of the consumer, user, or buyer?

In Shell there has been a shift in recent years away from identification by symbol towards identification by name. This has arisen because, often, local town planning regulations restrict the size of signs on petrol stations (Shell's main contact with the public). This has limited the long-range visibility of Shell stations to such an extent that the company has felt the need to use the name 'Shell' more strongly. This is interesting in communication terms because, while the symbol has become totally identified with an oil company, the word itself still retains much of its original meaning.

A big problem of any oil company is that it does not own all the petrol stations by which it is judged. The staff on Shell's 97,000 petrol stations are mostly not Shell employees but independent 'shopkeepers'. Just where contact with the public is closest, Shell's control is weakest. Yet, to a great extent it is the helpfulness of pump attendants and cleanliness of the station that influence customer attitudes to the company. Shell does everything it can about this, but it is no surprise that the company regularly engages in image research to check attitudes to the company. Such research has drawn out a number of factors that further complicate the problem.

For one thing, Shell is found to share certain image aspects with the oil industry generally and with all other oil companies. It shares certain attitudes attributed to all large companies, all international organizations, all western institutions, and with free enterprise and modern technology generally. This is only to be expected. But it is interesting that the relative weight of such things varies from country to country.

Not surprisingly, also, research has shown that numbers of 'subimages' exist, depending on particular points of view. Governments, trade unions, technicians, journalists, shareholders, and farmers each see Shell differently. The view differs, too, in developed countries and underdeveloped ones, in oil-producing countries and oil-consuming ones.

Despite the permutations, a definite Shell image exists. Research undertaken in many countries in Europe, the Far East, South America, and

Scandinavia shows that Shell is seen, in order of importance, as *international* (most countries see it as *the* most international oil company), *technically advanced*, *large* (often seen as the largest oil company), *American* (Shell is seen more as American than as Anglo-Dutch). *Powerful, old fashioned*, traditional, old established (often the longest established in a country, the Shell retail network can be older than its competitors), *trustworthy*, but *impersonal*, aloof, formal, austere, remote, distant, cautious, and less approachable than other companies; its products are seen to be *good quality*.

Other qualities noted seem at odds with these main findings. Australia and certain smaller South American countries see Shell as 'aggressive, pace-setting'. In France and Germany where Shell has made particular efforts in this direction, Shell is seen as having 'friendly, cheerful dealers'. In the UK, following special communication efforts over many years, Shell is often seen as 'relaxed', 'witty', and even 'cultural' (perhaps this goes back as far as Jack Beddington's prewar advertising policy of using the best British painters for Shell posters), a policy followed intermittently since.

From such research, Shell has drawn three conclusions. The first is that the public's image is fairly realistic. Images, they believe, are based on reality. To some extent they are a mirror reflection of the company. As G V Smith (the Shell International executive responsible for this project) said, 'A good image must be deserved by actual behaviour, and by communicating this behaviour.'

A second conclusion they draw is that the Shell image lacks individuality. Perhaps because the company is so large, so well known, it is seen in many countries to be nearly identical with the image of the oil industry overall.

While in people's minds Esso and Shell share a lot in common, there are distinct differences. Esso appears to be more democratic, fun-loving, youthful, popular. By contrast, Shell is seen as dependable, cautious, older, protective.

The third conclusion Shell have drawn is that some of the qualities attributed to them are positive, others are, at best, ambivalent. Bigness, for example, is good if it is associated with reliability, but may be damaging if it is related with being impersonal, monolithic, remote, less approachable. Whether bigness is seen in good or bad ways, depends on which particular market segment is being examined. The inference to draw from this is that it is a mistake to generalize and that Shell should analyse the particular attitudes of each important segment. The same is true of internationalism. While Shell's research shows mostly positive attitudes, there are people who equate it with 'foreignness' and think the worse of it for that. The answer here might lie in becoming more multinational in policies towards personnel and shareholding. The group believes it 'works awfully hard to be local with international experience'. An average of 98 per cent of staff are nationals of the country in which they operate. The central office of Marketing Communications handling corporate identity is only advisory, and the group gives as its reason for having no overall statement of communication goal that 'the identity objectives are set by each company in its own environment'. As evidence of this policy, Shell in South Africa is erecting a new building, Shell in Tokyo has just moved into new offices, and in neither case was the image aspect of these the concern of the central organization. 'We take it for granted that local management recognize the implications.'

Speaking of the corporate image generally, one senior executive of Shell International said: 'It may be better to be old-fashioned in India and modern in Brazil.' But there are obvious dangers here, and one wonders how practical this is. It is interesting that while Raymond Loewy's new work on stations will in his words 'provide plenty of scope for the use of local materials – timber in Finland, or tiles in Portugal and the Netherlands,' nonetheless, he hopes to find a design that will be acceptable worldwide. He added, 'We are not recommending rigidity or uniformity in its application,' but 'we do want to make the maximum use of modern building methods. . . .'

Notwithstanding its enormous activities in plastics (considered a separate business), farming, shipping, and the rest, the most important market segment to Shell is the motoring public. Because this public comes in closest touch with the company's products, service stations, and advertising, it is obvious that due attention must be paid to these visible manifestations of the company if Shell wish to maintain or improve their corporate communications.

Shell tends to attract middle and older age groups, middle and upper income groups, and owners of medium-sized and larger cars. If, as appears to be the case, people are attracted to certain companies because the images projected reflect some psychological need in themselves, the typical Shell customer might be thought to be responding to the more staid and conservative aspects of the image. (This is not so in the US where deliberate efforts have been made to revitalize Shell.) It is greatly to Shell's credit that they have pinpointed their public in psychological terms. From this information, Shell can judge its communication policies with greater precision.

Should the company want to widen their appeal to attract motorists who are younger, more dynamic and thrusting, they may feel the need to alter to some extent the visible manifestations of the company. This certainly appears to be an important aim of the new corporate identity policy. Loewy wants to attract the young, and to attract women motorists by offering them more fashion: 'Something elegant so they like to stop at Shell stations.' But since they've already seen that their existing image largely reflects the truth, they may want to shift some of their policies. The snag is that the reigning image is based on what now exists, its huge investments and policies built over sixty years. Shell is not new; it is successful.

To attempt to change the whole would be unnecessary and prohibitively expensive. Therefore, they have asked which segments of the market have impressions of the company which might be improved and how may this be accomplished? To widen appeal to satisfy everyone may result in broadening the base so wide that it means little to anyone. This must be a danger to any company so omnipresent; indeed this is partly the position now. Royal Dutch/Shell owns hundreds of companies and has interests in other marketing companies in a number of countries (in the UK, Shell Mex/BP and National Benzole; in Australia, Neptune; in Canada, White Rose; in Sweden, Koppartrans). It may be Shell's solution to shape the image of these companies to appeal more directly to people who do not respond to the stable, protective nature of the giant Shell. Indeed, National in the UK is positioned to be far younger and more thrustful. Shell executives say this is nothing to do with them, but perhaps it ought to be. This notion of recognizing one's own limitations and using another company to appeal to different markets, is extremely interesting.

Attempts have been made by responsible executives within Shell to re-define image objectives, to build on strengths, and to eliminate negatives. Designers have been retained, but the real change must come from within the group. A glimpse at the 1967 annual report *The Shell Transport and Trading Company Limited*, a publication not handled by the corporate identity people, gives no confidence that negatives have been recognized or acted on in that area. From the cover picture of an aerial view of the Rotterdam refinery, to a picture of a 20,000-ton tanker under construction, the emphasis is heavily, almost exclusively on their vast production capabilities. The last page of photographs is the first to show *people*. While there is a paragraph on 'personnel', which claims that 'they are the most important of our resources', the whole closely printed 36-page publication seems oddly impersonal. It may be argued that an annual report is not the place for image projection of this kind and is rightly kept away from group consideration. But is this true?

Annual reports tend to be used as an opportunity to present local problems and accomplishments. There is a case for bringing these within the province of the organization for corporate identity, as there is for considering buildings as an expression of the group. Shareholders are also motorists and customers. Staff who work in company offices form their opinions of Shell to some degree, by the place where they work. 'It's like a nightmare,' one employee said of the much criticized London headquarters. 'The corridors get longer every day.' This kind of comment cannot be irrelevant to any study of effective corporate communications.

A strong tide of fresh American thought appears to be sweeping through Shell International and it may be that a still stronger and more coordinated corporate identity will emerge. This is likely to be fresher, less rigid, more consumer-oriented. Michael Pochna, at Compagnie d'Esthétique Industrielle in Paris (the design office employed to handle the total problem – on a long-term, high-budget basis), points out that a corporate identity conveys quality 'not by rigidity or standardization. It conveys quality by having it.'

In the long run this may be thought more important in international relationships than attempts to be more 'local'.

The intention is to project a more favourable corporate identity than the present group image. More importantly, the company has attached a new value to the subject. The head of marketing communications at Shell International explained:

> In the past we've thought of design as visible manifestations only. The symbol and so on were *applied* to things. We think our VM is very strong but now we recognize that design runs much wider. We've become a marketing organization, and we have a concept of design for marketing running through the organization.

He sees corporate identity as 'a sort of umbrella' made up of three elements: how Shell looks, how it describes itself, how it really is. This is important. You get the image you deserve. So an essential point of the new Shell policy for corporate identity is that it is not confined to visual matters. Shell sees corporate identity as 'a powerful component in the business of surviving in an increasingly difficult world'.

A good deal has been written about IBM in this book. By appointing two distinguished consultant designers, and giving them the responsibility he has, the company president has created perhaps the most sophisticated corporate identity policy in the world. Design standards are very high. Concern with people is central, and well handled. Research into attitudes to the company and its business is, as we've seen, penetrating. The company's communication policies look better the more you study them. It might, therefore, be interesting to look at IBM in a little more detail to see how its design policies are handled in the field.

The company serves 104 countries, has 331 sales offices, 228 service bureaux, and 16 manufacturing plants. What happens? How are the policies of head office translated into action in the German, French, or British plants?

Does local management share the President's belief in corporate communication and high standards of design? What organization does IBM have to deal with these questions? Looking at the London office, the answer to the first question seems to be an unequivocal 'yes'. The standards are high. The managing director involves himself personally and often in the favourable expression of the company, even though there is an executive director responsible for communications.

The company, even at a local level, sees itself as a professional organization both in the sense of being good at its job and of feeling some sense of responsibility to society. But not for a minute does this intrude on the essential fact that IBM is there to make a profit.

The kind of organization used by IBM for its communication activity is rare, but likely to become more widespread. In London there is a communication division in which all the functions usually split into separate empires are integrated. These include advertising, design (three people), press relations, internal information, and audio-visual aids. All report to one manager.

The local design office designs or commissions the design of all sales literature, exhibitions, window displays, and individual assignments which bear on the corporate expression. A complete signing scheme for IBM plants and offices in the UK has been developed; all stationery used by the British company is rationalized into international sizes (effecting savings of £5500 ($13,200) a year). IBM's design policy is, in theory, overseen by two consultants several thousand miles away. How well does this work? How strictly must the local company adhere to centrally established standards? The policy seems fairly free and easy. The American consultant comes over once in a while, likes everything, and goes away. From the start IBM's corporate identity policy has been simple: use the logotype and do the best-quality work. Clearly, this could be open to a lot of interpretations.

A design manual was created in 1961, but it isn't used much. It is seen, at best, as a guide for the local design manager.

Not much attempt is made to coordinate the corporate identity or graphic design activity in different countries. Even though IBM standards are high, this apparent lack of active coordination may be questioned as a policy. IBM equipment is purchased by a small proportion of people who travel widely and read international magazines and trade journals, and so, in the interests of economy of effort it would appear to be right to coordinate all the special exercises. However, IBM don't bother too much about this. They feel that ideas vary in each country; that it is best to let a design manager create what he feels is appropriate to that country. In fact, attempts have been made to coordinate the design and production of literature internationally, but this has always failed for reasons of language, taxes, distribution, and design.

A second, more serious question arises when one looks at the coordination of functions. It is the company's policy to design products to a high standard. These are made on a 'one plant, one product' basis. In IBM's World Trade group there is one multinational, manufacturing policy. Plants in each country specialize in the production of specific machines or components. They supply continental rather than local markets. For example, data-processing equipment made in IBM's Scottish plant was shipped to over 100 countries in 1967. Because of this policy, product design must be closely coordinated. It is. Designer Eliot Noyes holds frequent coordination meetings between plants producing equipment. But there appears to be little connection between this design action and corporate identity action. The two functions are quite separate.

Equally, all the company's architectural and interior design (not only for itself but also for its customers) is also separated out. This is the responsibility of the estates division, which is not a part of the communications division. Advertising is in the same division as design, but not handled by the design manager (except in Germany).

A small example of the potential weakness of this occurred recently when the design manager established standards for laying out and typing letters and reports. He advocated using a single space after punctuation. But the equipment that may be used, IBM's MT 72, gives a double space. A small instance? Yes, but enough to suggest that less than the maximum use is being made of design skills.

IBM's former design manager in the UK thinks that the design team should comprise architects, furniture and interior designers, industrial designers, and designers of graphics and exhibitions, all closely coordinated.

This is not now the case in the US or anywhere else. This, incidentally, is the policy of Westinghouse, another company retaining Eliot Noyes. In 1967, it opened a 'corporate design centre' which, it was claimed,

> . . . will work to improve the appearance of everything the public sees from Westinghouse, be it product, building or printed literature. By combining the design operations and augmenting the design staff it becomes possible to use a calibre of design talent which no operating division could justify.

The centre is under a director of corporate identity. The last comment may explain why IBM sees things differently. It is a much more widely spread organization with offices bearing central responsibility even though they are not at the centre.

An important aspect of IBM's successful multinationalism is just this. IBM has rationalized its operations in Europe, for example, and divided output between manufacturing centres, setting up lines of command and moving work about to make the best use of its position in different markets. IBM has also decentralized in the US. Its 24,000 research workers, for example, are spread around 19 laboratories, close to manufacturing plants, handling practical development assignments. Apart from these advantages, they believe they wouldn't get the same performance if all their research were under one roof.

IBM understands the value of flow of information (Tom Watson Snr, who founded the company, never lived to see a computer, but he used the term 'data processing' forty years ago), and this knowledge has no doubt aided their multinational growth. For example, the company established IBM information services at Havant, near Southampton, to process internal information between various IBM headquarters, country organizations, marketing, manufacturing, and customer engineering. (The service is called 'RESPOND' which is an acronym built from *Re*trieval, *E*ntry, *S*torage and *P*rocessing on *O*n-line *N*etwork *D*ata.)

IBM is an outstanding company from the point of view of this book. Its phenomenal growth rate suggests, too, that its design policies are an attribute of successful modern business. Ironically, though, a company renowned for design can be open to attack if it fails in other ways. Unless performance is matched in all other areas – sales, service, and production – it can be accused of substituting imagery for reality, particularly by a dissatisfied customer. To this extent IBM takes great pains to be local. In IBM's French laboratory in the hills behind Nice, centre of all European research, 673 of the 700 staff are Frenchmen (the remaining 27 are probably specialists). In Britain IBM's chairman, Lord Cromer, is a former governor of the Bank of England, and it is claimed that all the staff and management are British. This most international company has an imperative instruction that companies should be as national as possible. While this may be so, one cannot help thinking that IBM's head office design policies (it must have more superb architecture than any other company on earth, and one of its machines is in New York's Museum of Modern Art), have had a major influence on attitudes to the company. This is true both in terms of making the technological age with which it is identified acceptable, and in making an American giant welcome everywhere.

15

How much to say

To quote George Santyana, 'Truth is like a diamond cut with many facets all of which can be set to advantage.'

What has been said up to now amplifies this view. We have been concerned with presenting an organization in its best possible light, but we've been complex enough to see that sometimes different audiences should be shown different facets. This itself distinguishes our point of view from that governing many corporate identity exercises today.

We've been at pains to say that any corporate identity activity should mirror the truth, and that graphic design activity should flow from a real understanding of the corporate ethos or structure. Any that does not will suffer from superficiality, and be as valueless as most superficial things quickly become.

Having satisfied this requirement, and having accepted that design and corporate identity work is of value, is it automatically right to spread the approved image with all the force at the organization's command?

Not everyone thinks so. Already we've seen the need to adapt and vary messages to suit local markets and particular market segments. And this, by itself, is an answer to those who see 'Global Communications' as the modern catch-penny cure-all.

Total information flow is unworkable. One must decide which facts to pass on, and which not to. From a total spectrum, different facts must be chosen to suit different conditions.

Accepting this, one accepts that communication is a matter of selection.

And then one sees that truth is, and must inevitably be, manipulated. Moralists would be right to take fright. But is there an alternative? Not silence, surely. Full and absolute truth all the time without omission or distortion is both impossible and undesirable. This has always been so. Every story, every conversation, every news report is a distortion of facts to create, optimistically, a greater truth because it is more readily comprehended. It is only the new ability to communicate, the massive media that reach into every home and every soul, that cast the dilemma in such a glaring light.

From a corporate viewpoint, the moral questions are real and should be dealt with seriously. Harshly put, the struggle can be between doing what is necessary to mislead no one, and doing what is desirable for the company.

Peter Gorb, an erudite, Harvard-trained British businessman who has long experience of the upper reaches of business, cites case after case to illustrate his view that there is an optimum level of communication beyond which it is wasteful and even damaging to go. The optimum, he stresses, may not be the maximum. This is important, because many people want to pour out good communications and good design without discrimination. The criterion is straightforward: To what extent does it contribute to the corporate objective?

First, he quotes the Oppenheimer situation: the scientist with twin loyalties, one to science, the other to his employer. If either loyalty is hurt, the other becomes ineffective. To subject a company scientist to the same flow of romanticized promotional material which it may be right for a salesman to receive, may be disastrous. It is better to spare him the communications, to let him work in the tranquillity of an undisturbed lab. Thus, we see how less-than-maximum communication can be good both for the transmitter and the recipient.

To take a specific example, it is interesting to look at Imperial Tobacco, one of the ten most successful companies in the world in terms of profits on assets, but now facing new problems.

In 1901 The American Tobacco Company bought into the British market. Astonishingly quickly, thirteen English firms (one at least going back as far as 1786) got together to resist the invasion. Together they formed the Imperial Tobacco Company. They were successful to the extent that next year (1902) the two declared a truce. American Tobacco agreed to keep within its own national boundaries, Imperial agreed the same, and together they formed British American Tobacco to tackle the rest.

The American Tobacco Company was split subsequently by the US Anti-trust Laws, and now Imperial holds a 28 per cent interest in it, and this affected the BAT agreement.

Through the years, Imperial Tobacco concentrated, more or less, on the industry it knows so well – tobacco. Its main outside investment, for example, has been, until recently, a sleeping 36 per cent of its main rival in the tobacco industry, Gallahers.

Confined to its own national boundaries by agreement, concentrated in one

(a)

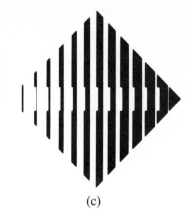

(b)

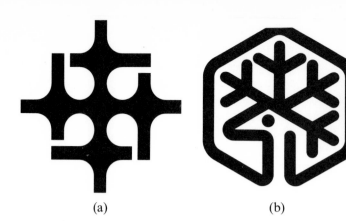

(c)

(g)

(h)

(i)

(l)

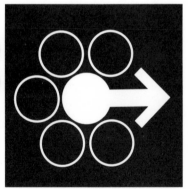

(m)

(n)

(p)

(q)

(r)

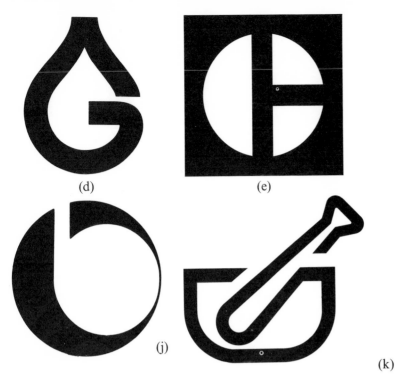

(d)

(e)

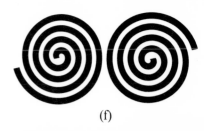

(f)

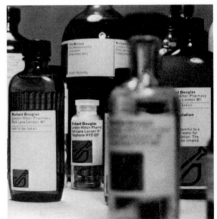

(j)

(k)

(a) Telerection TV aerials – Ulrich Haupt
(b) Zoological Gardens in Japan
(c) Pharmaceutical company in Japan – Hiroshi Olichi
(d) Grantham Rainwear – Clothing – Julian Swift
(e) Caterpillar Tractor – agricultural machinery – Lester Beall
(f) Van Gelder Papier – paper company – Karen Munck
(g) Mitsukoshi – Japanese department store
(h) Spar – retail group – THM
(i) Charrington United Breweries – brewery – David Wire
(j) Czech pharmaceutical company – Frantisek Boban
(k) Richard Douglas – pharmacy – Ian Bradbery
(l) Tate & Lyle – sugar refiners – Norman Jones
(m) David Brown – engineering – John Harris
(n) British Ropes – rope-makers – Frank Overton
(o) Marabou – Swedish chocolate manufacturer – Karen Munck
(p) Rohm & Haas Co. – chemical equipment – Lester Beall
(q) Lyons Bakery – packaged cakes and baked goods – Michael Russell
(r) International cultural exchange centre in Japan – Yoshio Amatani
(s) Bank of Montreal – Stewart & Morrison
(t) Borough of Lewisham – a borough of London – Geoffrey Woollard
(u) Smiths Food Group – food company – Karen Munck

Marabou

(o)

(s)

(t)

(u)

field, the name of the group was not inappropriate in days when names were less important.

But the UK market is a tough one for tobacco. Very high rates of tax make cigarettes so expensive that although sales figures are increasing, the amount of tobacco sold is not. Increasing concern about the health aspects of smoking also makes life harder for the company. Is it ethical to work for a cigarette firm? Some people won't. Should one invest in a tobacco company? Some people think not. Are sales of cigarettes and tobacco bound to decline as time goes by? It is not an unreasonable prediction that they will.

Increasing government legislation has hit Imperial Tobacco. At one time the cigarette-makers in the UK were spending an estimated £6 ($14) million a year on TV advertising alone. This has been banned. Other forms of advertising (Imperial spend about £8 ($19) million a year advertising various forms of tobacco) are severely controlled.

So for one reason or another, Imperial Tobacco finds itself with two-thirds of a £1500 ($3600) million market which is static or declining. Inevitably, it started to diversify.

Today, Imperial Tobacco is grouped into four divisions, tobacco, distributive trade, and general trade. Its first move into paper and board companies started as vertical integrations, supplying the packaging needs of tobacco. But today 70 per cent of the paper and board sales are outside the group. The general trade is mostly food. Investment here has been recent and heavy. Today Imperial Tobacco has 40 per cent of the potato crisp market (now at about £50 ($120) million a year). Competing with Heinz and others, it has 11 per cent of the baked bean market. It is the market leader in sauces (HP, Lea & Perrins), and is firmly placed in the canned fruit and vegetable market, frozen food, peanuts, and so-called 'snack food' market. New investments into the grocery business are virtually certain: the holding in Gallahers is being sold to make capital free for this purpose.

Evidently, the bulk of Imperial's business is still in tobacco. But, to some extent further development in that field would be damaging to itself, taking away from its own brands. Growth appears to lie elsewhere.

The food business they have taken on is extremely competitive – competition among giants – and Imperial Tobacco will need to take it very seriously to prosper. Its competitors now include General Mills, Heinz, Nestlé, and other big sophisticated grocery companies. Its distribution is not the traditional tobacco network Imperial dominates, but the younger, tougher supermarket operators. Its executives, no longer the cautiously developed Bristol or Nottingham men, but the new classless and highly competent marketing men.

For this situation, is the group name and image helpful or even appropriate? (The telegraphic address is, 'Smokes: Bristol'.) Until now, the group policy has been to concentrate promotion on brands, often backing them up with the assurance of well-established companies. Players, Wills, Ogdens, Churchmans, their subsidiaries, are all large, well-known and trusted companies.

Golden Wonder, marketing potato crisps and nuts, is newer but as well known. In the grocery field, HP Sauce, well known in Britain, was bought last year for £22 million ($52,800,000). Smedleys, one of their canned food brands owned by National Canning, is well known. Through their large investments in British American Tobacco, Imperial have an interest in cosmetic firms Yardley and Lentheric, and the ice cream company, Tonibell. They also own companies making pesticides, plastics, teaching machines, and textiles, as well as ladies' hairdressers and toy shops. To this extent, the group name, 'Imperial Tobacco', is unrelated to its marketing or diversification policy. Research shows that Imperial Tobacco is known as a tobacco company by its investors and others, but not credited with the products it sells; that people associate it with some products it doesn't make. Is this company/branch policy enough? Investors, after all, look for the assets and profits of the group.

Should the group change its name? Should it make more of its non-tobacco interests? Should it bring up the group identity as a common link between member companies? At present this happens only slightly. Member companies are not anxious to emphasize their connection with competitors in the group. Indeed it has been said that the best-kept secrets are those which Wills' keeps from Players' and vice versa.

In straight competitive terms this is understandable, though the group claims it is increasing internal information on less contestable matters.

Should consumers be made more aware of the group's widespread activities? Imperial seem to doubt it. They tried producing a symbol some years ago and looked at over 100 sketches. But the idea seemed to founder on a simple question: How many more cigarettes will it sell? 'Shareholders know us backwards,' they say. And that they consider important. This may not be the sole criterion of a corporate identity or even an important one, and it is probably true that Imperial Tobacco seems an inappropriate name now and will probably become more so in five or ten years' time. But the group may rightly think that it works sufficiently well where it matters. This could be an interesting example both of the complexity of such questions and of the wisdom of aiming at an optimum level of communications which may be less than total. Nothing in corporate identity work says you have to appeal to everyone, though a judgement on which audiences to include and which to omit is a delicate one. It is worth recording that since this was written Imperial Tobacco has introduced a new symbol, based on the corporate initials.

The question raised about the corporate name is interesting and plainly relevant to discussion of corporate identity. It is surprising how seldom companies are prepared even to consider altering their name. It can be done, as we've seen: US Rubber, in less than two years effectively changed their name worldwide to UniRoyal because they felt the existing one was inadequate. But this is rare. Though a reluctance to change a name known and established is proper and easy to understand, the idea should not be ruled out. If giants can change universally known names, then smaller firms have still more freedom.

Reverence for a name, oddly, is combined with a lack of understanding of its ability to convey ideas. They may be accidents of history (Tunnel Cement, after an ancient tunnel near the company's first North of England works), or created to identify functions (Globe Electric Tram Car Co., in Milwaukee, which no longer makes trams and has changed to Globe Union); picked just to identify (after the founder, Olivetti); or made up (Kodak); or to describe the product (Volkswagen, Frigidaire); or to convey impressions (Betty Crocker, General Dynamics); or describe the corporate purpose (International Business Machines, now reduced to IBM, General Foods, Scandinavian Airlines System, London Transport).

Some of these stand the passage of time better than others. Some names currently in use are inappropriate to the corporate purpose and must act against it. Ample evidence suggests that companies change their business and their products, and words change their meaning. Characteristics once thought advantages can become liabilities. The last point was exemplified when the Bowery Savings Bank changed to the New York Spending Bank, to counter words which it felt had become unhelpful. Rio Tinto-Zinc, a British mining company of immense size, mines a wide range of metals worldwide, but it has nothing to do with Rio Tinto (site of an old mine), and zinc is only a minor part of its production. The true scale of the company is probably little recognized.

A case can be made for many companies to look anew at their name, from an image standpoint. The more specifically a name is related to a variable, the shorter its constructive life may be.

The case for giving careful thought to this when new companies are formed is incontestable. Yet too often the name of a new company, particularly in a merger situation, appears to be chosen either by lawyers or to satisfy the ego of the participating principals. Neither is right.

Consultants were working in British Motor Holdings, considering their corporate image, when the company merged with Leyland. The name chosen, British Leyland Motor Holdings, is a mouthful which can't survive, and was thought by the design consultants to be incapable of consistent application. At that time it was directly counter to the international image advice being given by the specialists. But they weren't asked.

A matter as important as a corporate name should be chosen skilfully not to pacify or impress, but to accomplish defined image objectives. Of course, it is the senior executive's task to take the long view, and this may differ from what seems right in the immediate situation.

In most organizations hierarchies exist which face different goals. The senior executive looks forward five years, the middle only one year, the lower level may have objectives to be reached in one week or one month. Sometimes these goals are different in direction and even conflicting. Some people believe it right to tell everyone the long-term goal, unvarnished.

Others say this is too simple, and may prevent staff from reaching short-term goals. It may even be said that people lower down an organization can't know the subtleties of some problems and may draw wrong or even harmful conclusions by being told them.

For years we have heard of the follies of withholding information from employees. Joint works councils, and attempts to enforce worker participation at board level, are examples of efforts being made to widen the flow of information. But it is interesting to ask whether any union trouble in a plant has ever been caused by management revealing too much too soon.

In today's climate this thought is sacrilegious. But it is interesting to ask, and may lend further weight to the 'optimum' view of communications. Peter Gorb says:

> A question to ask is this. To what extent can you provide information that will damage the ability of people to do their jobs properly and accomplish the objectives set out for them?

He argues that, 'every communication is a suppression of information'. This is done, he points out, by selection and emphasis. Just as it is neither possible nor desirable for people in lower positions to be told everything, neither is it possible for people higher up to know everything. There is just too much to absorb and it, in turn, may damage a man's ability to reach his objectives. Selection is necessary. Knowing what information to select can be crucial. Many bad decisions are made by people who receive wrong information.

On a different tack one can add a further human restriction to good communications. We are victims of our environment. We grow up to accept certain standards and impose them on our business and on others. And it may be that the cultural framework for the business created this way can actually be damaging to it. Examples abound of just this situation. Any cooperative enterprise, any firm, places limitations on the people in it, as a violinist is limited in an orchestra. And one tends to employ people who accept similar limitations. In this case communication may be easy. But the middle-aged, white-collared executive who employs youths with long hair (because the business requires mavericks) will find communications difficult. They will be, too, if the same executive has young people for a market. This situation is common today.

If, as has been claimed, 'no man can escape his culture', this a real handicap to easy, full communication.

Chester Barnard[1] claims that an organization must be *effective* in terms of achieving the goals it sets itself, and *efficient* in doing so by providing the maximum satisfaction to the people helping to accomplish the goal. Here can lie another cause of conflict, another reason for considering corporate communication in a more thorough way. Are the satisfactions sought by the foreman the same as those pursued by the sales director? If not, how do they differ? And how can the flow of information help each of them? There is a case for controlling the dissemination of information so that it will do good and not do harm. There is an argument in favour of deciding what information to dispense to whom, and recognizing that profound variations exist.

This book has been about one aspect of corporate communications, establishing the effective corporate identity. The whole subject is being taken seriously by industry and government the world over. Companies of all kinds, dealing both locally and internationally, have established offices of corporate identity and are developing coherent policies. Others will do the same. Believing in this, the author has run the risk of overstating or over-simplifying the case. It is well to reaffirm that not all communications are good, neither should it be assumed that the more you say the better you are. Indeed, one of the few rules we've learnt is that there are few rules. For any organization, there is an optimum level of communication activity. To do too much, with a basic faith in the virtue of democratic awareness, could possibly be as damaging to corporate goals as to do too little.

Whatever has been said, therefore, must be related, constantly, to helping to accomplish corporate goals. A discriminating approach to the subject is needed. From the days of overcautious secrecy, to the new, often naïve attitude that frank communication is good for its own sake, must emerge a subtler, more precise recognition of what is needed, how much, where, and when. In all these questions design plays a central role.

The final reminder must be that there is a dynamic to corporate identity work. The job is never finally done. This book has largely been about finding the right course to plot and how to set off safely. No one expects to sail the seas without looking often at a compass. Winds, tides, currents, rocks, and other vessels give cause for frequent adjustment. Corporate identity work, the expression of a corporation to its public, is affected by as many obstacles. It is imperative, therefore, to consider this work as continuing and long term.

This means maintaining and enhancing standards of performance as time passes to suit the dynamic of rising discrimination. It means checking the results of one's actions. The company is a moving body in a shifting world. Relationships alter imperceptibly, constantly. All organizations should see that they receive (and instigate formally) a regular flowback of information. Communications are thus two way: from the customer and others to the company; from the company to its audiences, in endless adjusting relationships.

The need for this is apparent enough. In our changing times, 'it is not,' Peter Drucker has said, 'necessary for a company to grow bigger. But it is essential it constantly grows better.'

If this book helps anyone do that it will have done its job.

REFERENCE

1. *Functions of the Executive*, Harvard U.P., 1966.